ART
OF
Entrepreneurship

Published by:
Lotus Press : Publishers & Distributors

ART OF Entrepreneurship

A.K. Banerjee

Lotus PRESS

4735/22, Prakash Deep Building
Ansari Road, Darya Ganj,
New Delhi-110002

Lotus Press : Publishers & Distributors
Unit No. 220, 2nd Floor, 4735/22, Prakash Deep Building,
Ansari Road, Darya Ganj, New Delhi- 110002
Ph.: 32903912, 23280047 • E-mail : lotus_press@sify.com
www.lotuspress.co.in

Art of Entrepreneurship

ISBN: 978-81-8382-276-3

Published by : **Lotus Press,** New Delhi-110002
Printed at : Concept Imprint, Delhi

PREFACE

Entrepreneur is presently at the crest of popularity, increasing number of educated youth, are getting attracted towards entrepreneurship and are starting new ventures. The various school of management have realized the reality and have focussed their attention to the concept of entrepreneurship and the art of creating new ventures. The liberalisation of economy and resultant increase in competition, role of managers have catch up the attention of yours youths. The theme of entrepreneurship helps the young entrants to understanding their traits and attitudes to be developed, make them responsible for preparing business plans, seek financial help from different financial institutions and make them able to run business on profitable lines.

The simple of entrepreneur is who creates his own business, who organizes, operates and share the risk of business. The entrepreneur is a person who perceives an idea and then bring together man power, material and arranges necessary capital needed for business. Entrepreneurship is a creative and innovative response to the environment, he is a person who processes of setting up new ventures. Entrepreneurship is a composite skill that is a mixture of many qualities and trails such as imagination, risk taking, ability to harness factors of production, land labour, tecimology and such other various factors. Thus, entrepreneurship culture implies a set of values, norms and traits which are conducive to the growth of entrepreneurship. It is the organizational culture that deals with new business opportunities and creation of new set-up, looks for ways and means to capitalise on new opportunities and controlling the related matters.

This book deals with the topics of—*Concept of Entrepreneurship; Origins of Entrepreneurship; Characteristics of Entrepreneurship; Qualities of Entrepreneurs; Entrepreneurial Development in India; Social Responsibilities and Obligations; Emergence of Entrepreneurial Class; Types of Entrepreneur; Entrepreneurial Training; Entrepreneurial Behaviours and Motivation; Entrepreneurial Development Programme; Search for Location;* etc.

I hope that students and those in the education field will find it useful for academic and competitive examinations. I owe a deep sense of gratitude to my publisher for materializing my present endeavour.

Editor

CONTENTS

1

CONCEPT OF ENTREPRENEURSHIP

The spirit of enterprise makes man an entrepreneur. Such a spirit transformed him from a nomad to a cattle rearer, to a settled agriculturists, to a trader and to an industrialist. Thus, entrepreneurs are persons who initiate, organize, manage and control the affairs of a business unit what combine the factors of production to supply goods and services, whether the business pertains to agriculture, industry, trade or profession. Entrepreneur is the central figure of economic activity and propeller of development under free enterprise. Agricultural or industrial development is brought out by entrepreneurship. The development or underdevelopment is the reflection of the development or underdevelopment of entrepreneurship in the society.

Different writers defined the entrepreneurial functions in different ways. Cantillon was the first to use the term entrepreneur. He portrayed an entrepreneur as one discharging the function of direction and speculation. J.B. Say, moving along in the French (Cantillon) tradition was the first to assign the entrepreneur a definite position in the economic process. His contribution is summed up in the pithy statement that the entrepreneur's function is to combine the factors of production into a producing organism. Such statement may indeed mean much or little. He certainly failed to make full use of it and presumably did not see all its analytic possibilities. But to Adam Smith, the father of Political Economy, the entrepreneur was a proprietary capitalist, a supplier of capital and at the same time working as a manager intervening between the labour and the consumer. Adam Smith also treated him as employer, master, merchant and underaker, but explicitly identified him with capitalist, probably in view of the English economic background. David Ricardo, a contemporary of J.B. Say, supported Smith's approached and treated the industrial manufacturer and agricultural farmer synonymously as entrepreneurs throughout his famous book "The Principles of Political Economy and Taxation." In his words, "the farmer and the manufacturer can no more live without profit than the labourer without wages." According to Ricardo, the prime motive of the entrepreneur is to accumulate and without motive there should be no accumulation to facilitate capital formulation and economic development. He also stressed that the motive for accumulation will diminish with every diminution of profit and will cease altogether when profits are so low as not to afford an adequate compensation of the risk and trouble which the entrepreneur encounter in employing his capital productivity. John Stuart Mill emphasized the function of direction that the function require "no ordinary skill." F.H. Knight propounded the theory that the entrepreneur are a specialized ground of people who bear risks and deal with uncertainty.

According to Schumpeter the defining characteristic of the entrepreneur is innovation. The function of the entrepreneur falls into a sequence of three inter-related activities: *(a)* perception of the opportunity based on an innovation: *(b)* promotion of business organization capable of embridging the innovation and *(c)* running the business unit as a going (profitable) and growing concern. The above manner of splitting of the entrepreneurial function, however, leaves certain basic areas to be analysed and understood. In his view the term innovation is only a short-hand expression for a range of decisions that the entrepreneur must be capable of making. The decisions might be in the fields of technology, organization, selling and markets, research, public relations, employment, coordination of production inputs and even management, the functions which is clearly beneath the entrepreneur in Schumpeter's view.

Modern interest in the entrepreneur as a key figure in economic progress stems in large part, as is well-known, from the work of Schumpeter. In Schumpeter's system, entrepreneurship is essentially a creative activity. The entrepreneur is the innovator who introduces something new into the economy. The innovation may be a method on production not yet treated by experience in the branch of manufacture concerned, or a product with which consumer are not yet familiar, or a new source of raw material or of new market hitherto unexploited, or other innovations in the strict sense of term. According to him entrepreneurs are business leaders and not simple owners of capital. They are men of vision, drive and talent, who spot out opportunities and promptly seize them for exploitation. By virtue of their initiative, earnestness and activity they accomplish significant advances in national production and incidentally obtained a good slice of the increasing national income as reward for their untiring efforts in the from of profits which they consider as the barometer of their success. Personal gains constitutes the spur of economic activity under private enterprise. In furtherance of their interest, entrepreneurs undertake business ventures and economic activity involving new combinations of factors of production which rise the level of productivity resulting in better utilization of resources. Hence, entrepreneurs constitute the generating force of motive of economic development, Schumpeterian view implies that labour supply, resources, existing capital and the estate of arts only create potentiality for capital productivity, while it is the enterprise which performs the miracle of transforming the potential into effective productivity. As the entrepreneur is the sovereign of productive activity and the key to economic development, it follows that a substantial part of the explanation of differences in levels of investment between the developed and underdeveloped countries and between different states in the progress of any single country is to be found in the size, energy and scope of operation of the entrepreneurial class. It means that the degree of vigour of the entrepreneurship maters much in determining the level of economic activity. Schumpeter's innovation entrepreneur represents the most vigorous type of enterprise. But the Schumpeterian entrepreneur is a rare species in underdeveloped countries and the paucity of entrepreneurship, both in quality and quantity, is a patent fact in the areas. It is sometimes said that this type of entrepreneur is needed in underdeveloped countries. Thus. Prof. Dupriez writes: The type of entrepreneur who exploits possibilities as they present themselves within a limited time-horizon and mostly on a small scale the entrepreneur of J.B. Say can only produce limited results. Society must produce Schumpeterian innovators with a long time horizon and capable of achieving substantial transformations.

Unfortunately such innovators and rarely found in underdeveloped countries, and precisely because the countries are so underdeveloped. In the words of the ancient proverb chosen by Marshall as the motto of the Principles, Nature Non-facit Saltum. A country with little or no industrial tradition can hardly produce the innovators capable of substantial transformations without first producing, and in large numbers, the humbler type of entrepreneurs. Economy-shaking innovators, like great scholars, are the exceptional few who emerge at the summit of a broadly based pyramid. Such men do not appear and could not function until a certain level of educational, social and technical progress has been achieved. They are at once a product a development and an agent of further development. But the need for Schumpterian innovators in countries which are beginning to industrialize must not be over-stressed. The technologies and products needed by these countries have already been developed in more advanced countries. Men are needed who can adapt these technologies and products to the particular conditions of less advanced countries. These countries primarily need, not innovators, but the "imitators" who even on Schumpeter's system are primarily responsible for transforming the forward step of the pioneer into a magnitude of economic importance.

The importance of these humbler entrepreneur who "exploit possibilities as they present themselves and mostly on a small scale" must not be underestimated. In the first place such adaptation requires no mean ability. It often involves what has aptly been called "subjective innovation, that is, they are able to do things which have not been done before by the particular industrialist, even though, unknown to him, the problem may have been solved in the same way by others. Establishment and successful operation of a manufacturing enterprise in underdeveloped countries often require such abilities as well as considerable resourcefulness in adjusting to the changing circumstances which characterise developing countries. Men capable of doing so are in short supply and contribute much to the economic development. The enterprises may be small and unimpressive when judged by the standards of more developed countries. But their success points the way for others and given the high propensity to imitate, which exists in less developed areas, can set in motion the chain reaction which leads to cumulative progress. There is much truth in the statement that the most important ingredients in the so called "favourable climate of entrepreneurship" in countries which stand at the threshold of industrialisation, is the example set by a significant number of businessmen successfully engaged in certain activities, particularly in manufacture. There is another reason why the humbler type of entrepreneur is important in underdeveloped countries. These countries are placing great stress in their economic planning on the development of medium and small scale industries. There are sound economic reasons for this in countries where capital is scarce, investors cautious, markets severely limited because of low purchasing power and entrepreneurs largely inexperienced in the ways of industry. In addition, many countries aspire to a decentralised industrial structure in which ownership and economic power will be distributed widely. In India, this goal has become a corner-stone of economic policy. This small and medium scale industries have an important role to play in the world's poorer countries.

Notable among the studies of such humbler entrepreneurs are those of James T. McCrory, James J. Berna and several of UNESCO. McCrory's study is confined to small enterprises in a North Indian Town, whereas Berna's study centred round medium scale engineering enterprises in Tamil Nadu and Coimbatore cities. The UNESCO's studies covered small enterprise in selected regions like Mumbai, Howrah, Delhi, Rajkot, Hyderabad and Ludhiana. Such of the studies prompted the writer to undertake the present study of entrepreneurship in industrial estates, of course, with special reference to the Coastal Region of Andhra Pradesh. Whether it is small or medium enterprise, inside or outside the industrial estate wherever such a humbler type of entrepreneur is found, he is the person who brings into existence a new industrial enterprise either alone or in collaboration with others. As rightly mentioned by Berna "he is, perhaps, rather a pedestrian figure by Western standards: an adapter and an imitator much more than a true innovator, a man who has much more in common with Marshall's organizer of the factors of production than Schumpeter's creative disturber but in a poor country attempting to industrialise, a potent, change producing figure, nonetheless."

Like other developing countries India considered industrialisation as the basis for creating a better economic order for its citizens. For a variety of reasons, industrial policies followed by successive governments were such that the desired impact was either not there or was only visible for fleeting movement. A study of the human factor in industrialisation is, therefore, called for. The central figure in this study is the entrepreneur and its role in economic development with special reference to Gujarat industrial development. Informal aspects such as centrality, integration, practivity, creativity, helping relationship, personal growth, confrontation have been studied and argued into existing knowledge.

The entrepreneur is a very contentious subject in economics as well as. in social sciences. Now-a-days, it has become the subject of multidisciplinary. Few scholars have agreed on the place that should be given to the entrepreneur in formal economic logic. Everyone though is agreed that...'by ignoring the entrepreneur, we are prevented from accounting fully for a substantial portion of our historic growth and our body of theory as it has developed offers us no promise of being able to dial with a description and analysis of entrepreneurial function. Penrose reinforces this by stating that Enterprise or Entrepreneurship, as it is sometimes, called, is a slippery concept, not easy to work in formal economic analysis, because it is so closely connected with the temperament of personal qualities of individuals.

Penrose thus indicates the complexity of the subject by indicating the overlap between economics and the other disciplines such as sociology and psychology. The research student must, therefore, study these other disciplines and to decide whether the methodology utilized elsewhere can help in determining aspects of the entrepreneurs hitherto unknown. Recent ideological and religious trends need to be taken into account, if only to determine their impact on entrepreneurial performance. In a given social mileu cultural factors are difficult to ignore. Entrepreneurs given the complexity of human beings, have managed to defy any kind of quantification scholars have failed to arrive at consensus of their attributes or activities.

During the last three decades, the concept of entrepreneurship has assumed prime importance both in, research and in action for accelerating economic growth in the developing countries. Attempts are being made to inculcate the spirit of entrepreneurship among people who are likely to turn into manufacturers, or are likely manufacturers, and to facilitate the activisation of entrepreneurship through the organization of support system such as capital assistance, technical know how marketing of goods, management and many other infrastructural facilities. The economic development of a nation is sparked largely by its enterprising spirit. The characteristics emerges from the interplay of behaviour and activity of a special segment of the population known as entrepreneurs. If the nation's economy is not to stagnate under the ministrations of professionals, it must be continuously revitalised by the infusion of new energy, new ideas, and nucleous for economic growth. The greater emphasis is still on the development of entrepreneurship in small manufacturing units in the expectation that it will multiply employment opportunities, minimize inter-sectoral and inter-regional imbalances, and had to a more equitable distribution of income among the people of varied social strata. The building of modern nations depends upon the development of people and the organization of human activity; Capital, natural resources, foreign aid, international trade, of course, placing important roles in economic growth but none is more important than manpower. The academicians—economists, psychologists, sociologists, social psychologists, anthropologists, political scientists and historians alike and also the State, have gradually recognized the importance of entrepreneurship as a major determinant of the rate of economic growth. A fact that industrial enterprise and economic growth are correlated and the activity of an entrepreneurs is necessary for launching an industrial enterprise has now become obvious to all. The findings of social science research should be of great significance in designing programmes of action for developing entrepreneurship. However, because of diverse findings regarding the factors that contribute to entrepreneurship, there is no consensus among social scientists about the strategy to be adopted for its development. Theories indicate that entrepreneurship is the result of jointly of ethical value systems, need for achievement motivation, socialization process, community character and industrial and political milieu. The use of these findings in designing action programmes for developing entrepreneurship raises many issues, such as: Is it feasible to change ethical value and motivation? How much time may it take to change them? Whether a change in them could necessarily generate entrepreneurship? How much time does not involve? Can a society afford to bear such cost? It is really difficult to change the ethical values, the community structure and the achievement motivation of people. There have been some efforts on art of planners and researchers to inject entrepreneurial motivation of people, and managerial skill into entrepreneurs, both potential and actual, but the results have not been very encouraging.

One of the reasons for the partial failure of action programmes was that the theories of entrepreneurship were not understood in their proper context. Most of the theories, which are taken as the basis for designing action programmes, were developed in a historical and macro-level situation. They did not consider the individual entrepreneur in the micro-level situation of the manufacturing unit. These theories, no doubt, provide deep insights into the historical process and macro-level cross sectional comparative analysis of entrepreneurial growth, but they lack in comprehensive understanding of entrepreneurship and its functions and correlated at the unit level. Of late, efforts are being made to analyse entrepreneurship and its correlates in an organizational setting. Such endeavour would provide deep insights for designing action programmes and the present study has been conducted in this hope. Assuming that the action programmes may be guided by the theoretical knowledge that was available, it was decided to explore existing research on entrepreneurship and its implications for action programmes in order to identify the gap between research and action for developing entrepreneurship in an organizational situation and to suggest research and action these objectives, a contingent model has been developed in this study.

The 'Entrepreneur'

The affluence of a nation may be judged by its ability to produce useful goods and services and to distribute them widely throughout the population. The question arises, what factors under gird the process of building economic wealth? Some countries, notable several in western civilisation, have built a wealth economy, while others, even though they have comparable climates and resources in raw materials, have not achieved similar success. Historian and economists have not always toward national wealth. One consistent theme appears to in the literature on the wealth of nations, however, it points to a special class of individuals who have been the initiators of economic growth. These persons are known as entrepreneurs. The natural habitat of entrepreneurs is small business. They are rarely found in giant industries. When a company grows beyond some critical size, its increasing complexity forces it to replace its venturesome founders with professional managers who are not usually noted for their inventive, risk-taking behaviour. They are rather the guardians and conservators of the *status quo.*

"The definition of the entrepreneur is one of the most crucial and difficult aspects of the theory. There are two main approaches to defining anything; the functional approach and the indicative approach. In the context of the entrepreneur Casson says quite simply that 'an entrepreneur is what an entrepreneur does.' It specifies a certain function and deems anyone who performs this function to be an entrepreneur. The indicative approach provides a description of the entrepreneur by which may be recognised. Unlike a functional definition, which may be quite abstract, and indicative definition is very down-to-earth. It describes an entrepreneur in terms of his legal status, his contractual relations with other parties, his position in society, and so on. The entire structure of the theory developed rests upon the following definition 'an entrepreneur is someone who specialise in taking judgemental decisions' about the coordination of scarce resources. In principle, the entrepreneur could be a lanner in a socialist economy, or even a priest or king in a traditional society. In practice through, entrepreneurship is closely identified with private enterprise in a market economy."

Entrepreneurs, in the modern sense, are the self-starters and doers who have organized and built successful enterprise since the Industrial Revolution. Those who wish to start their own business can benefit from studying the characteristics of entrepreneurship. Understanding the psychological profile of the entrepreneur, they can judge whether they fit the pattern and have a reasonable chance for success in starting a business of their own.

Kilby has likened the entrepreneur with a rather larger and very important animal called 'Haffalump' hunted by many individuals, but all unable to capture him. All claim to have been seen him and have variously described him, but wide disagreements still among them on his particularities. Thus, the term 'entrepreneurs' has a plethora of definitions, but no consensus has to date emerged on what skills and abilities a person should possess to become an entrepreneur, how can entrepreneurial class can be developed, or how the supply of entrepreneurial persons in a articular society can be increased. It may appear a little surprising that despite the subject of entrepreneurship have been under discussion for more than two centuries, the concept still remains a little clouded. Entrepreneurs, on the other hand, are quick to see possibilities for achievement. They are not blinded, as managers in large, staid organizations often are, by the ingrown culture in which they are embeded. Entrepreneur do not suffer from the trained incapacity often professional, to use Theorotein Veblen's tronic term. All definitions of entrepreneur are in terms of his function. From centillon who coined the entrepreneur in the early 18th century to the social scientists of today; the emphasis in varying degrees has been on the function or the other of the entrepreneur.

Hoselitz point out that these definitions have, at one time or another, been associated with:

(a) Uncertainty-bearing;

(b) Coordinations of productive resources;

(c) Introduction of innovations; and

(d) The provision of capital.

Richard Cantillon, an Irishman living in France, called entrepreneur as one who buys factor services of certain price and sells his product at uncertain price, thereby bearing a non-insurable risk. J.B. Say expanded the term, and bringing together of the factors of production, provision of continuing management as well as risk-bearing were including in entrepreneurial function. Adam Smith treated him as provider of capital, but not playing a leading role.

The first major work on entrepreneurship came from Schumpeter. It was published for the first time, in German, in the fall of 1911 and an English version thereof appeared in 1934. The put the human agent at the centre of the process of economic development and regarded an entrepreneur as one who, through new combinations of means of production, carries out the introduction of a new good, the introduction of a new method of production, the opening of a new market, the conquest of new source of supply if raw materials or half manufactured goods, and the carrying out of the new organization of any industry.

It is this definition which received the widest comments and has been a subject of considerable debate, the academicians swinging either pre or anti-schumpetarian. A spate of contributions on entrepreneurship appeared from Research Centre in Entrepreneurial History at Harvard. But no unanimity could still emerge either on entrepreneurial functions or conditions governing supplying of entrepreneurs. A various definitions of 'entrepreneur' came from the academicians of the developed nations and at a time when the problems of the Third World had not received so much attention. And therefore the theoreticians took a very restricted view of entrepreneurial functions. They never thought that the entrepreneurial functions, would change for time and place they could not conceived of any entrepreneur who would have perform multiple functions in an under-developed economy, an economy where virtually and kind of activity is entrepreneurship.

A clearer view of entrepreneurial functions started emerging only when some of the social scientists dabbled in economic history and some others undertook explorations in some economics. Recognizing the problem not to speak of the Schumpetarian innovations, even initiative entrepreneurs had a distinct role to play. They provide, he feels, a fillip to the process of economic growth, sometimes having as strong or perhaps even stronger an impact on economic growth as real or alleged innvoations. Even the multiplicity of entrepreneurs, lacking in creative enius of inventors, but possessing all other characteristics of successful entrepreneurs, is desirable for under economics. The term 'entrepreneur' still remained vague and was being identified with the firm. It was still a matter of controversy, whether entrepreneur was a group of an individual. Most theorists did not envisage an entrepreneurial group. As an entrepreneur was treated to be an individual, it was presumed that one who launched an enterprise, would continue to associated oneself. Therefore, launching of the enterprises and not the ongoing organization received their comments.

The controversy was further accentuated with the emergence of large corporation in which ownership and control allegedly became distinctly separate functions and the identifications of the entrepreneurs got blurred.

Another dimension was added to it by the organization theorists who, in order to explain whose objectives an organization represent, treated as an entrepreneur or a single strategist or a coalition composed of a large number of participation with widely varying preference orderings ultimately resulting into a joint preference ordering through bargaining and side payments.

In modern times, organizational part thus come into sharp focus. The term has gained such a wide currency that anyone routinised act is regarded as entrepreneurial act in the same way as every discipline in being is being called science and every systematic activity, an industry.

An extensive sketch of the potential scope of the entrepreneurial task in an under developed economy has, however, been recently provided by Kilby. He envisages that the entrepreneur himself might have to perform the following kinds of activities for the successful operation of his enterprise :

(a) Perception of market opportunities (novel or initiative)

(b) Gaining command over scarce resources

(c) Purchasing inputs

(d) Marketing of the product and responding to competition

(e) Dealing with the public bureaucracy (concessions, licences, taxes)

(f) Management of human relations with the firm

(g) Financial Management

(h) Management of customer and supplier relations

(i) Acquiring and overseeing assembly of the factory

(j) Industrial engineering (minimizing inputs with a given production process)

(k) Upgrading, process and product quality

(l) Introduction of new production techniques and products.

Some of the activities in Kilby's list are such as can be parcelled out to competent lieutenants, but that will depend upon the scale of production, the degree of development of the high-level manpower market, social factors governing the amount of responsibility with which hired personnel will perform and the entrepreneurs' comparative efficiency in utilising high-cost managerial employees. It is a known fact that a vast majority of firms, in underdeveloped countries, are of small and medium-size, and factor input markets are also under developed. Therefore, the demand placed upon the entrepreneurial unit are considerably more extensive in low income as compared to high income economies.

Thus, the entrepreneurial roles may encompass all activities from the perception of economic opportunity to the external advancement of the firm in all its aspects. Certain tasks demand the entrepreneur's critical attention, whereas others cell for little, and can be safely delegated to subordinates. Hence, different settings may warrant markedly varied entrepreneurial personalities.

❋❋❋

2

ORIGINS OF ENTREPRENEURSHIP

The more significant findings in this chapter will be considered in the light of existing theory and of the actual world of the entrepreneur rather than being abstracted from Secondary Sources. Reference to concepts developed in other disciplines will also be made. There are many number of ways in which the world of entrepreneurs may be interpreted. To consider their development from the point where they enter industry is to use an arbitrary point of reference. Much has happened in the economic and psychological life of the entrepreneurs to take them to the brink of a new era. What is it that takes them to the cross-roads of life and to accept significant risks? There is much cumulative experience given that any individual is unique. Some of the origins mobility, experience, education and training of entrepreneurs will be examined and the informal influences of family, caste and community and their effect in the making of entrepreneurs will be discussed. The aim here is to examine entrepreneurs in as wide a context as possible. The geographical spread of the sample was the entire length of India.

Entrepreneurial activity needs an environment conducive to its growth. It involves assumption of considerable risks by the entrepreneur and, therefore what is essential is "entrepreneurial security."

(*a*) the nature of the physical environment; its location in terms of trade, military and naval necessity; its characteristic; its position, whether continental or maritime;

(*b*) technology;

(*c*) institutions or organizations like State and law; church and sect (In their power aspects); social organizations and social classes; the character of political institution as well as the stability of the social structure; and

(*d*) "ideological" or "sentimental" (attitudinal) security like nationalism, legalism, religious feeling or spirit, and social attitudes which may or may not favour entrepreneurial action.

In the same vein, Cole also speaks of environmental conditions which influence the origin of an entrepreneurial class:

(*a*) stable government;

(*b*) external security; protection from war and invasion etc. and

(*c*) internal security; protection from internal strife and revolution, protection of person and property under law, and the assurance of legal process in disputes.

Any analysis of the industrialization process within a country and of the concomitant behaviour of the entrepreneurs needs, therefore, a study of the interplay of a host of such factors. A complex economic and social behaviour such as entrepreneurship can scarcely develop in an unfavourable setting. It is only where the ideal market conditions have been most closely approximated in terms of political, economic, social and ethical securities, that economic change has been most free from restraint?

Business Communities Prior to the Advent at Modern Industry

The Indian society from times immemorial has been characterized by a kind of stratification into religious and regional sections. The Hindu society was conceived as 'home hierarchius' where caste groups rigidly separated from each other on functional basis a feature which perpetuated the practice of following the family occupation leaving little scope for mobility between one occupation and another. Among the Hindus, the *bania* was such a caste which mainly dealt in commodities and carried on money lending business. As the *banias* specialized in trade and commerce, they were the most urbanized section of the community and because of their financial predominance enjoyed an enviable position in the urban centres, though in the caste-hierarchy they came third after the Brahmins and the Kshatriyas, where the caste system was relatively loose, the danger of ostracization absent and the trading castes missing, people of other, castes also moved into these occupations and came to be regarded as members of the business community.

By the middle of the 19th century, India had a fairly developed business community, Gadgil notes that Gujarat and erstwhile Saurashtra were the most urbanized and developed tract in the whole of India with a continuous record of foreign trade lasting over centuries. This region had a highly developed *bania* community, both Hindu and Jain and also large Muslim trading communities (Bohras, Khojas and Kacchi Memons), mainly converts from Hinduism. Apart from trading chiefly in cotton, piece goods and merchandize in their own regions, they participated very actively in maritime trade, both to the West with the Persian Gulf, Arabia and Africa and to the South and Southeast along the coast of India to Malaya, Indonesia, etc.

Parsis who migrated from Persia and Gujarat in the 8th century were chiefly noticed as artisans, carpenters, weavers, etc., in the 17th century. They had become prominent shipbuilders by the 18th century and had setup merchant houses in Bombay, Burma, China and London. Their overseas trade was mainly in yarn and opium. They also acted as brokers for the European traders at Bombay (Now Mumbai) and Surat and gradually, established themselves as merchants and traders of repute. By the middle of the 19th century, they had emerged as a dominant trading and financing community of Bombay and Gujarat. Thus, the Parsis and Gujarat trading castes became the wealthiest Indian communities by the middle of the 19th century, controlling whatever foreign trade was in Indian hands.

Among the trading castes of South India were the Chettis sub-divided into various groups such as the Telugu Komatia, the Tamil Nattukottai Chettis, Beri-Chettis, etc. The Komatis were the chief traders not only in the Telugu districts, but also in Mysore Coimbatore, Canara and other places. The Nattukottai Chettis were the chief bankers and financiers of South India. The Beri Chettis traded chiefly in drugs, grain and cloth. In the beginning of the 19th century, they were described as respectable kind of pedlars travelling in caravanas. These trading communities also had their trade connections with the South-East Asian countries like Burma, Ceylon, Malaya, Singapore, etc. The Chettiars formed an important part of the propertied class of Indians in Malaya. They built-up connections with reputed Indian business firms and acquired landed and other investment interests. They had become indispensable as the principal purveyors of rural credit. The Nattukottai Chettiars in particular were prominent in Burma. More than half of their total working funds, or three-fifths of their working funds invested abroad, were employed in Burma.

On the west coast in south, most of the trade was in the hands of Syrian Christians called Nazrani Mappilas and Mohammedan merchants known as Moplahs. The internal trade of Cochin and Travancore was financed mainly by the Nazrani Mappilas, while the Moplahs were found in larger or smaller numbers throughout Malabar and Canara. In Canara, the Moplahs shared the functions of trade with the Konkania who also conducted the banking business of the country. As the trading monopoly of the East India Company faded and finally vanished after 1857, many of the Christians prospered as merchants in the benign atmosphere of victorian free trade. They became private bankers, and when native joint stock banks began to appear at the end of the 19th century, it was the Syrian and Chaldean Christians who were most active in promoting them.

In Bengal, the situation was slightly different. There did exist communities like the 'Subarna Banika' who traditionally specialized in trade and commerce and corresponded to the *banias* in other regions. The Bengali merchants and capitalists did participate in trade, industry and banking along with their British principals, but as the British political power became more firmly consolidated, the Bengali houses gradually receded from the scene. The Bengali merchants' capital then turned towards the land, as investment in land had become profitable. The average Bengali received English education and joined mercantile house us well as administrative services. Thus, the educated upper and middle classes of Bengal were rendered not prone to enter the risks of trade and commerce. If at all people from communities such as the Brahmins and Kayasthas in Bengal entered business, it was to assist and act agents of British businessmen. Hence, Bengali names in business are relatively unimportant and where they occur, they are mostly of the rising professional agent class and not those of indigenous trading elements. There was another important and fairly developed business community called 'Marwaris', hailing from Marwar in Rajasthan. The trading and money lending Castes attained their greatest development in Gujarat and Rajputana through which lay the famous trade route from the

Gujarat ports to the historical centre of the Great Mogul State. But even during the first half of the 19th century, Rajputana was raveged by feudal strife and it was by no means an ideal place for large scale trading and money lending operations. Further, although local trade was relatively brisk, its volume remained fairly constant and that afforded only limited scope for the merchant's capital. Therefore, the situation as it developed in Rajputana necessitated the trading and money-lending capital to seek new opportunities beyond its borders. They spread their tentacles in towns throughout the north, east and west, especially the commercial centres of Bombay (Now Mumbai) and Calcutta (Now Kolkata). They carried on their vocation unassumingly and consolidated their position in these centres. With the rise of British Commerce, they gradually replaced the Bengalis as the British agents in Calcutta. The Brahmins and Kayasthas of Bengal who earlier served as the British agents drifted into landed proprietorship and the learned professions, but the vacuum so created was filled by the Subarna Banika. But, in the meantime, Bengal became a hot-bed of politics which was not palatable to the British ruling and commercial elite. Wherever possible, a Bengali was replaced by someone who promised to be more dependable. And in this affair, the Rajasthani traders proved to be much more cooperative than Bengali commercial castes.

Besides these trading and moneylending communities and the European commercial interests, there were some others like Bhaties and Lohanas who were engaged in local trade and were very widely dispersed all over the country. A vigorous urban Hindu community called "Khatris" was engaged notably in trading activity not only, in Punjab but also in Afganistan, Central Asia, etc. In the absence of *bania* elements in Maharashtra, Yajurvedi Brahmins and Chitapavan Brahmins took considerable part in trading, moneylending and indigenous banking.

Emergence of Business Communities as a Source of Industrial Entrepreneurship

In the middle of the 19th century, the British economy was undergoing a metamorphosis. The industrial revolution was having its profound impact, and forcing the British industry to search for wider markets. Consequently, the British thought of developing India into a market for their manufacturers and exploiting her natural resources to their advantage. To penetrate into the Indian territory, they undertook the building of certain infrastructure such as the development of the ports of Calcutta and Bombay, construction of roads, and laying down of railway lines. The Indian economy could no longer escape the consequences of transformation taking place in the governing country.

This considerably enlarged the extent of the Indian market and the trade with Britain grew. A growing number of people were drawn towards trading and import-export which had become highly profitable. The control of the East India Company on trade had become loose during the middle of the 19th century. Its own employees, civil and military, set up their independent businesses with finances borrowed from the company, their acquaintences and the businessmen in England whom they represented in India. This brought the native businessmen in exceedingly close contact with the British businessmen. As a boon to them came the blockade of the southern ports in the American Civil War which shut off Lancashire's supply of raw cotton. The result was that the cotton price in India touched a new high and the profits made by her merchants were far in excess of their wildest dreams. Now a wave of speculation overwhelmed them and for many a mart the temptation to multiply his gains was so treat that the boom attained the character of a 19th century South sea Bubble. Gold and silver poured into Bombay in such profusion that the legitimate channels of investment were soon exhausted and the money overflowed into a multitude of crazy concerns.

The railways were introduced in India in 1853, but a network was still to be built. The problem of industry was not merely the assembling of raw materials at the factory site or disposing of the finished products, but the very of a factory coming into existence was a serious matter. The entire machinery and know-how had to be imported from England. At the time, there was no Suez Canal, all the machinery had to be imported by sailing vessels *via* the Cape, the operative had to be thoroughly trained and the industry had to meet the farmidable competition of English manufacturers. Under the circumstances, any industrial activity was the result of venturesomeness. Thus, in the early stages of development, the businessmen were faced with two dilemmas: on the one hand, they were strongly motivated to search for alternate avenues of employment for their surplus fund accumulated in trading and on the other cautious and calculating; is they were, they would not risk their money in hitherto unknown ventures. Further, modern industry was not on cottage or household basis but on factory basis, not based on the use of manual power but on mechanical power and called for attitudinal adjustments, heavy investment and knowledge of machine operation.

Amongst the native people, there were certain classes of persons who could possibly be influenced to take to industry. There was the Indian mercantile class along with the European that had taken advantage of the rapidly expanding trade and amassed considerable riches in trading, financing, import-export, financing of the armies and winning the favour of the rulers. They were familiar with the availability of raw materials, market for their products and also to a limited extent, management of resources. However, certain cultural, social and economic factors militated against their coming to industry. They had, no doubt, enough funds for investment, but no technical competence. They did not know much about the administration of factory labour. As they were already engaged in highly lucrative trading, there was no lurement to abandon their former places in the business and social order.

The Brahmins who also constituted a small part of the business community preferred to take to administrative services which were then becoming more important and were akin to their hereditary occupations. The Mohammedan group spent their incomes extravagently and had little capital to invest. Another class of persons who could be possibly influenced to take to industry were craftsman who had recently been uprooted from their vocations by the factory products of England and had become a burden on land. They knew manipulation of raw materials, but had virtually no capital to invest, were illiterate and ignorant of the complexities of the new machines and processes, and had little ambition to make money. They did not dream of wealth and even if they had indulged in such visions, they would have preferred the certainty of their hereditary occupations, with hereditary customers and social relationships, to the uncertainty associated with so radical a change from all their traditions and experience.

No facilities for technical education existed at that time and hence, the technician entrepreneur was not even within the real of imagination. There were no layers of mechanics of technicians or engineers in whom the spirit of entrepreneurship could permeate. The other classes of people who did not come from mercantile background but had accumulated money were not ready for entrepreneurial activity. With the development of transport and communications during the second-half of the 19th century, the land values in urban areas were showing signs of rapid rise. The professional men and salaried officials who had savings to invest found it more attractive to put most of it in landed property a very safe and sound investment. An investment in industry does not seem to have been a very strong motive with the rejahs, maharajahs, nawabs and zamindars, barring a few exceptions. They preferred to hoard large quantities of precious metals and indulge in conspicuous consumption on a very large-scale.

It was, therefore, out of these various classes of people, a short and logical step for those merchants who had been successful in purely trading pursuits, importing manufactured goods and exporting raw or partly processed raw materials, to look round for profitable ways of using their growing capital resources and begin to commit their savings and the savings of their friends, to the establishment of those industries for which India seemed to offer a promising field. The conditions were favourably disposed to the merchant class and among them, to the community which was close to the British and in a position to hire the British technicians. This is how the Parsis came to set up their first industrial ventures and were able to make a transition to modern industry. It was but natural for the Parsis who came into association with the Europeans, adopted their ways of life, spoke their language, to take advantage of the situation. As they were eminently fitted to be means of transplanting European manufacturing to India and also all the essential requisites of industrial development existed at Bombay, the Parsis came into the vanguard of this movement and set up the first industrial ventures.

The development of cotton and jute textiles was a natural corollary of the fact that India was the home of hand manufacture of both cotton and jute and so, there was great familiarity with these fibres and skill in handling them, besides large home production of the raw materials. For these industries, factory machinery and organization had already been brought to a high degree of perfection in other countries. Moreover, India was a very great consumer and importer of cotton cloth while the world's commerce was furnishing a rapidly expanding market for jute bagging and wrapping material.

The history of modern industrial enterprise dates back to 1854 when the first successful textile mill was setup at Bombay by a Parsi gentleman named Cowasjee Nanabhoy Davar—a financier and trader having many British contacts. The mill was styled as the Bombay Spinning and Weaving Mill. He was soon followed by Ranchhodlal Chhotalal, C.I.E., a Sathodra Nagar Brahmin, in 1859 when he established the first mill at Ahmedabad under the name and style of the Ahmedabad Spinning and Weaving Mills. Simultaneously in 1855, the first jute mill came into existence at Rishre, a few miles above Calcutta, due to the enterprise of an Englishman named George Acland, but owing to financial stringency, the mill had to be closed down in 1868. However, fortune smiled on George Handerson who started the Borneo Jute Company in 1859. These early enterprises were so successful that the Bombay Spinning and Weaving Mill declared in the very first year of its existence a bumber dividend of 20 per cent.

Inspired by this initial success, the other enterprising Parsi and Gujarati cotton traders who had reaped huge speculative gains during the American Civil War (1861-65) also made their debut in manufacturing and one textile mill after another was set up at Bombay and Ahmedabad. After 1875, there was a veritable boom, the number of mills in Bombay Presidency increasing to 41 by 1877 and in India as a whole to 51. Several up-country mills were established during this period. Besides growth at Ahmedabad and Kanpur, a beginning was made at Sholapur and Nagpur. By 1884, it is surmised, the number of mills in the country was not fewer than 63 with a total nominal capital of Rs. 65.76 million and the number rose to 156 with a total nominal capital of Rs. 141. 95 million at the torn of the century. The progress registered in jute mill industry was no less spectacular. Handerson's venture was a success from the very beginning and his performance led to the establishment of three other mills in quick succession—two in 1862 and one in 1866. From 1868 to 1873, the five mills except the Rishre Mill made huge profits.

Thus, India stepped into the modern industrial are during the latter half of the 19th century. A new caste termed by Lamb as the 'British Caste' appeared and dominated the industrial scene on the north-eastern side. With the weakening of control of the East India Company and after gaining familiarity with the Indian Market, the servants of the Company, civil and military, started, acting as agents for the businessmen in England and later, launched enterprises on their own. They developed coal mining, tea plantations and jute manufacturing industries. The jute industry remained predominently under the control of the British till the Indian participation appeared after about 70 years. On the western side in Bombay and Ahmedabad, the Parsi and Gujarati traders rest content with the manufacture of cotton textiles.

Absence of Broad-based Entrepreneurship

The history of growth of entrepreneurship in India leaves many questions unanswered. One is left guessing about: why were not people from other backgrounds attracted to industry, despite the fact that the roots of industrialization had already been laid? Why could not the spirit of enterprise permeate among other sections of the society once the success of the initial enterprises was demonstrated by the Europeans and the Indian business communities? Again, why did it concentrate in a few families even among business communities? The explanations for absence of broad based entrepreneurship are commonly found in caste system, the inertia of associated cultural traditions, joint family system and the like.

Besides, unlike Japan, the commercial development did not stimulate the agricultural sector of India's economy. Most of them were engaged in subsistence farming, and the new economic opportunities did not interest the wealthy farmers. To participate in trading and manufacturing enterprises and search for new sources of profits, as the Japanese wealthy farmers did, did not fascinate them much, as even otherwise they enjoyed a better social status. Thus, on the one band, the moneylenders squeezed the masses and on the other, the landlords, nawabs, rajahs and maharajahs (excepting a few who did make industrial investments and provided concessions to their subjects) who were patronized by and served as agents of the British government, dissipated their resources, indulging in conspicuous consumption and hoarding wealth in the form of land, gold or jewellery. The problem was further accentuated by the lack of banking and communication facilities, as the scattered bits of savings could not be mobilized. Thus, the whole political and economic system was such that the foreigner, the landlord, and the moneylender took the economic surplus away from the peasentry, failed to invest it in industrial growth and thereby ruled out the possibility of repeating Japan's way of entering the modern era.

The educational system was so geared as to turn out clerks. No importance was attached to development of technical abilities or executive skills. The enterprises for a long time continued to be supervised by Europeans. In the industries owned and controlled by foreigners, appointments of native to managerial and higher technical jobs were kept to a minimum. Even as late as 1900s, the State Policy was biased against technical education on the ground that the prevailing pattern of employment opportunities did not justify its encouragement. The legal profession and administrative services attracted the most brilliant and highly ambitious young man. As the government did not ascribe any high value to economic development, society continued to bestow the greatest prestige on intellectual or non-material pursuits. Further, as the liberation movement gained momentum, many talented young man drifted toward political activity.

The process of industrialization could be hastened through certain instrumentalities like an ideology of industrialization and, more specifically, active State policies calculated to foster growth. In fact, the kind of entrepreneurial development that took place before Independence was a product of the situation created by the State itself. None of the policies which the situation called for emerged. As the relevant decisions were ultimately determined by the interests of the British economy and the British private capital in particular, the State pursued a *laissez-faire* policy despite public demand for State action to protect Indian industries. It is evidence by the fact that though cotton textile was a highly profitable industry, the British themselves took to an industry which would not compete with their home industry. Even later the overwhelming bulk of foreign capital investment-accounting for the bulk of the total investment in modern industry was in transport and extractive or export industries for the economy of the colonial country, such investment merely meant the growth of enclaves, their linkages effects being confined to a minimum.

It was not a problem of mere State inaction or indifference; it was a calculated discrimination, perpetrated against the Indian industrial interests, which scuttled the growth of native entrepreneurship. The dominance of modern industry by the European business houses before the First World War was supported and reinforced by a whole set of administrative, political, economic and financial arrangements within India. The European businessmen very consciously set themselves apart from native businessmen they claimed a cultural and recial affinity with the British rulers of India which was denied to the Indians who might compete with them. Even in such petty matters as railway facilities, it was pointed out in testimony before the Acqorth Committee in 1919-20 that the Indian subordinate railway officials were able to capitalize on the chronic shortage of care by exacting payments from Indian businessmen in return for prompt service, whereas British business expected and received prompt service on the Indian railways without paying bribes to petty officials. The same practice was virtually conceded by the Wedgewood Committee in 1937. The fact that the British business for whose interests the government existed, had easier access to government *i.e.,* all matters militated against the growth of native entrepreneurship in general. But the emergence of widespread entrepreneurship was also hampered by collaboration between the native business interests, the foreign interests and the alien government.

For many things, the industrialists have to depend upon the State. The State is a big buyer of many products and can influence the market. Those who came in touch with the State, established a rapport and cooperated, considerably increased their gains and influence. There was no class of men more interested in the stability of the British rule in India than that of the respective merchants. Even when the national movement started, they served simultaneously both the motives of pursuit of profit and sympathy with the movement. Noboru is surprised that time Indian entrepreneurs were able to separate their economic and political activity to enable their own communities to prosper. In fact, the resourceful always maintains special connections with the government as it can affect his opportunities of profit, but others who lag behind, suffer.

Family relationships are directly important, for they decisively extend the capital available to the individual promoter. But wider ethnic connections are fully as significant. In an unstable economic and social order, decisions often rest on personal judgements of a man's trustworthiness. Derivation from a known background, membership in a proper church reputation for virtues defined in accordance with standards accepted by the ethnic group are of inestimable importance in this respect. Keeping these considerations in view, membership in a trading community has significant advantages for industrialists in making, community members tend to trust each other, especially since most communities impose sanctions against violators of other code of behaviour, community membership facilitates raising capital. The confidence among community members widens the pool from which accountants, managers, technicians and partners can be drawn. It is difficult to trust outsiders in a situation fraught with uncertainty, with few institutional or professional standards, and with no traditional code of ethics in industry. Entrepreneurs from a trading community can also often draw on information and a wider circle of trusted collaborators than can others do. The Indian trading of trusted communities had very well-knit resource groups and the members not belonging to these trading communities were not only at a serious dis advantage in these regards, but also were not very welcome to an exclusive preserve of theirs.

3

CHARACTERISTICS OF ENTREPRENEURSHIP

The characteristics of an entrepreneur that contribute success are the result of his achievement motivation. McClelland discussed the following qualities or characteristics of a successful entrepreneur as: a person with technical competence, initiative, good judgement, intelligence, leadership qualities, self-confidence, energy, attitude, creativeness, fairness, honesty, and emotional stability.

1. *Mental Ability.* Mental ability refers to intelligence and creative thinking. An entrepreneur must be reasonably intelligent, and should have creative thinking and must be able to engage in the analysis of various problems and situations in order to deal with them. The entrepreneur should anticipate changes and must be able to take decisions.

2. *Human Relation Ability.* The most important factors contributing to the success of an entrepreneur are emotional stability, personal relations, consideration and tactfulness. An entrepreneur just maintain good relation with his customers. He must also mainrtin good relations with his employees as he is to motivate then to perform their jobs at a high level of efficiency.

3. *Communication Ability.* Communication ability is the ability to communicate effectively. Good communication also means that both the sender and the receiver understand each

other and are being understood. An entrepreneur who can effectively communicate with customers, employees, Supliers and creditors will be more likely to succeed than the entrepreneur who does not.

4. *Clear Objectives.* An entrepreneur should have a clear objective, the nature of the goods to be produced and subsidiary activities to be undertaken. A successful entrepreneur may have the ability to make profit.

5. *Business Secrecy.* An entrepreneur must be able to guard business secrets. Leakage of business secrets to trade competitions is a serious matter which should be carefully guarded against by an entrepreneur.

6. *Technical Knowledge.* An entrepreneur must have a reasonable level of technical knowledge. Technical knowledge is the one ability that most people are able to acquire if they try hard enough.

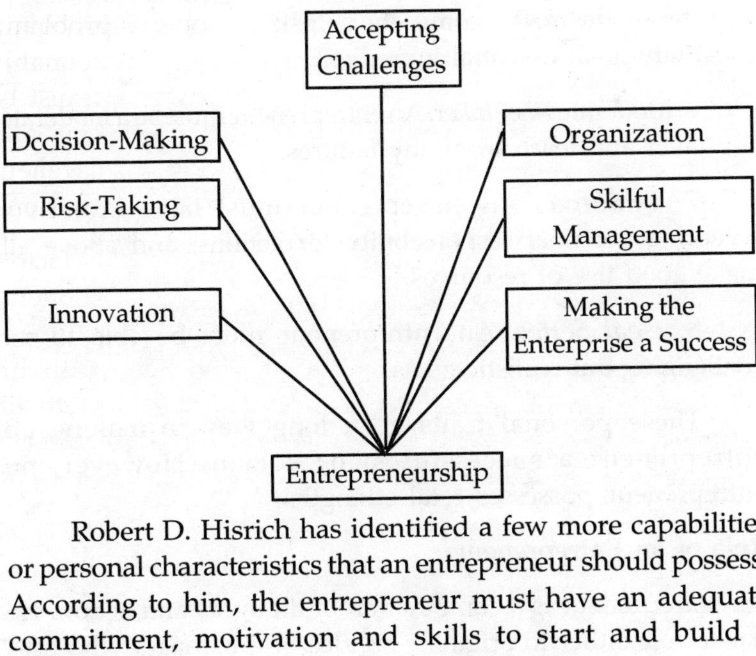

Robert D. Hisrich has identified a few more capabilities or personal characteristics that an entrepreneur should possess. According to him, the entrepreneur must have an adequate commitment, motivation and skills to start and build a business. The entrepreneur must determine if the management team has the necessary complementary skills necessary to succeed. Some key characteristics of successful entrepreneur are:

1. *Motivator.* An entrepreneur must build a team, keep it motivated, and provide an environment for individual growth and career development.

2. *Self-confidence.* Entrepreneurs must have belief in themselves and the ability to achieve their goals.

3. *High Energy Level.* Success of an entrepreneur demands the ability to work long hours for sustained periods of time.

4. *Long-term Involvement.* An entrepreneur must be committed to the project with a time horizon of five to seven years. No ninety-day wonders are allowed.

5. *Persistent Problem-Solver.* An entrepreneur must have an intense desire to complete a task or solve a problem. Creativity is an essential ingredient.

6. *Moderate Risk-taker.* An entrepreneur must be a moderate risk-taker and learn from any failures.

7. *Initiative.* An entrepreneur must have initiative, accepting personal responsibility for actions, and above all make good use of resources.

8. *Goal Setter.* An entrepreneur must be able to set challenging but realistic goals.

These personal traits go a long way in making an entrepreneur a successful man/woman. However, no entrepreneur possesses total strengths.

Role of an Entrepreneur

An entrepreneur is a combination of thoughts and action. He has to role either to originate an idea or a manager who tries to improve by initiating productive changes. His main role is to take up factors of production and employ them to produce new products and services needed by the society.

Once Jules Buckman rightly said "Basically, the entrepreneur sees a need and then brings together the manpower, material and capital required to finance the proposed venture".

1. *Introduction of Change.* An entrepreneur's role lies in introducing the following five broad types of changes:

(a) Initial launching, *i.e.,* original production of goods.

(b) Subsequent expansion *i.e.,* increase in quantity.

(c) Factor innovation, *i.e.,* increase in the supply or productivity of factors mentioned below:

— Financial (procuring capital from a new source or in a new form).

— Labour (upgrading existing labour)

— Material (procuring old material from new source or use of new material).

(d) Production innovation, *i.e.,* changes in the production process.

(e) Market innovation comprising of changes in the size or composition of the market, *e.g.,* production of new goods, change in the quality or cost of existing goods, discovery of new markets etc.

Basically, the entrepreneur always searches for change, responds to it and exploits it as an opportunity to become leader in that line of product.

2. *Addition in Productivity.* Entrepreneurship has a role in raising productivity. The keys to higher productivity are:

(a) Research and development,

(b) Investment in plant and machinery and human resources,

(c) Resource allocation from areas of average to above average rate of remuneration of capital and labour, and

(d) Realization of internal and external economies of scale.

3. *Innovation.* Entrepreneurship plays a significant role in promoting innovative technologies, products and services. Invention of zipper, titanium, operation of spinning jenny from foot to steam engine, invention of power loom etc., owe to the spirit of entrepreneurship.

4. *Innovator.* He is a man who is known for introducing something new product, a new technique of production, opens new markets, exploits new sources of raw materials and capital.

5. *Fabian Role.* They are very serious and careful in adopting and implementing any change. They are very careful about new development and if need so, these changes can be effected without delay.

6. *An Able Organizer.* An entrepreneur brings together various factors of production. He coordinates and controls the efforts of all the persons engaged in his enterprise. He harnesses land, labour, capital and other resources for the benefit of mankind. Therefore, an entrepreneur is an organization builder.

7. *Dream Creation.* Dream creating gives entrepreneurs the energy and desire to become involved in its execution. During dream formation every area should be tailored to the situation with the objective of having the entire organization ultimately own the dream.

8. *Man of Vision or Man of Risk Bearing Capacity.* Risk is an inherent and inseparable element of entrepreneurship. An entrepreneur guarantees rent to the landlord, wages to workers, and interest or dividend to the investors. He assumes the uncertainty of future.

9. *Gap Filling.* The gap between human needs and the available products and services gives rise to entrepreneurship. An entrepreneur identifies this gap and takes necessary steps to fill the gap. He introduces new products and services, new methods of production or distribution, new sources of inputs and new markets for this purpose.

10. *Dynamic.* Entrepreneurship is a dynamic function. Entrepreneurs thrive on changes in the environment which bring useful opportunities for business. Flexibility is the hallmark of a successful entrepreneur.

Functions of an Entrepreneur

The following are the main functions of an entrepreneur:

1. *Determine Objectives.* An entrepreneur decides well in advance the objective of an organization and concentrate his entire energies for achieving these objectives.

2. *Development of the Organization.* Entrepreneur is responsible for organizing different clements of an enterprise and to see the whole process of production and sale goes as per specification.

3. *Arranging Technology and Equipment.* An entrepreneur is required to arrange the needed technology and equipment for the smooth conduct of an enterprise.

4. *Securing Resources.* Entrepreneur is a person who arranges initial capital and further additional capital as per need. Excess or deficit capital both situations are bad.

5. *Development of New Markets.* An entrepreneur is to focus the pattern of demand of various consumers as these

days products are manufactured as per the demand of consumers.

6. *Good Relation between Public Authorities and Society at Large.* In the present day set-up entrepreneur is supposed to link the interest of business leader to the interest of consumers or society, as these days business leaders understand their social responsibilities.

7. *Financial Management.* Large scale business needs crores of rupees thus to arrange such huge amount is not a joke, the excess or deficit finance than the needed amount may be dangerous, therefore, a meaningful balance be made. Adequate finance is needed for the success of an organization.

8. *Management of Human Relations.* Industries peace cannot be imagined unless, human relation are not taken care.

9. *Production Management.* An entrepreneur is responsible for balanced production management. The production schedule should flow as per schedule, this will cater the need of consumers without delay.

Barriers in the Path of Entrepreneurship

Vesper has listed 12 main barriers in the path of entrepreneurship. These are as follows:

1. Lack of viable concept
2. Lack of market knowledge
3. Lack of technical skills
4. Lack of seed capital
5. Lack of business know-how
6. Complacency (lack of motivation)
7. Social stigma attached to certain vocations
8. Monopoly-protectionism

9. Job "Lockins", "Golden Handcuffs" or attachment with the job.
10. Inhibitions relating to patents
11. Time Pressures, distractor
12. Legal constraints

Some of these barriers are due to specific personality traits called 'personality quirks', entrepreneurs make them hard working.

Problems/Barriers/Impediments to the Development of Entrepreneurship. There are societies which are more entrepreneurial than others, such societies promote entrepreneurial behaviour with which are the net result of more entrepreneurs in such societies. The importance of entrepreneurship to the society in general and its economic development in particular. In general, there are certain factors which either support entrepreneurship or act as barriers to the entrepreneurship, such factors can be (1) economic, (2) social, (3) political (4) psychological. The negative influence create inhibiting milieu to the emergence of entrepreneurship. These barriers can be economic and non-econmic.

Environmental Barriers to Entrepreneurship

(1) Economic

(2) Non-Economic

(a) Social

(b) Personal

(a) Capital

(b) Labour

(c) Raw Material

(1) *Economic-Barriers.* These can be:

(a) Capital. Capital is the most important pre-requisite for setting up the new enterprise. Capital is a lubricant to the process of production. Money is the resource that helps mobilise other resources like men, materials and machines. Entrepreneurship in any society increases with the increase in the supply of capital. Thus, lack of availability of capital with any society or nation acts as a serious barrier for promoting entrepreneurship in that society.

(b) Labour. Cheap labour of a developing country may prima facie appear to be strength in promoting enterprises, but the fact is that cheap labour is often unproductive or has a low level of productivity. This unskilled and low productive labour acts as a barrier in setting up the modern enterprises. However, by using labour saving innovations, the innovative entrepreneurs have been able to overcome the disadvantage of high cost labour in developed economies.

(c) Raw Material. In the absence of raw material no enterprise can be established and in the absence of enterprises the entrepreneurs do not emerge.

The lack of raw materials is normally the greatest economic barrier for growth of entrepreneurship. Japanese society has been able to overcome the problem of lack of raw material through innovative management systems.

(2) *Non-Economic Barriers.* A large number of sociological and psychological factors act as non-economic barriers. Many societies and regions endowed with skilled labour and natural raw material have remind entrepreneurially backward because of such factors. The factors which prevent the emergences of entrepreneurs can be classified as environmental and personal barriers. The environmental barriers are rooted deep in the society and are also known societial barriers.

(a) Cultural Block/Social Block. People are bound by their cultural values. Every society lays down some unwritten

norms of acceptable behaviour. All members of that society are required to follow these norms. If such norms are broken, the society does not approve of the resultant behaviour and exert direct and indirect pressure on the individual to conform to a particular way, purely because it is customary. Ground rules of social behaviour are learnt from the parents at a very early age.

Practical Values. Most of progressive societies, discourage day dreaming, playfulness and fantasy by their adult members. Such behaviour is considered childish and unsuitable for grown up persons. The adults are required to be functional in their thinking.

Emotional Block. Entrepreneurship involves risk, besides financial risk it involves emotional risk. Every entrepreneur runs a risk of making mistakes and incurring losses in his venture. People usually understand two situations *i.e.*. either a person is right or wrong. Throughout one's life one is trying to find right answers to the problems and avoid the wrong solutions. Right answer is considered synonymous to success and being wrong is considered as failure. A fear of being wrong leads one to construct elaborate justification for own judgments and actions.

At work, people use a number of productive tools like sales forecast, market research; budgets etc., so that in case of failure their decisions are perceived as rational. In case the decision proves to be wrong one can defend it by claiming that high level of prudence was exercised. People are afraid of not only making mistakes but more so appearing foolish because of such mistakes. This emotional fear is the barrier to entrepreneurship.

(b) Personal Barriers to Entrepreneurship. In a given environment few people take up the career of entrepreneurship. Even among the societies wllich are considered entrepreneurially progressive only selected few

venture to setup their own enterprises. This indicates that personal barriers prevent people from launching their enterprises.

The following factors act as a personal barrier to entrepreneurship development:

1. *Lack of Sustained Motivation.* Most people enjoy initiating a new product. People generally have a need for new experiences and involvements. Being a part of new development furthers their status need. They appreciate the idea of being a part of something new. Thus, it is easy to attain a high level of commitment, enthusiasm and motivation at the initiation stage of an enterprise. However, when the project is off the ground or faces first obstacle the initial level of interest gradually wanes off. The entrepreneurship requires a sustained level of motivation and commitment and it is often difficult to sustain this motivation against the initial hurdles.

2. *Inability to Dream and Use Sub-conscious.* It is general experience that when a deadline is fixed for an assignment, the initial progress is slow and gains pace when the last minute approaches. Most people do their best work immediately prior to the final deadline as they allocated enough time in the early stages of the assignment to store up the information in their sub-conscious. That is why when one faces a difficult problem, one is advised to "sleep on it". This recognizes the power of sub-conscious, the under-used part of one's intellect. The entrepreneur needs to use both parts of his intellect, the sub-conscious for incubation of ideas and conscious for resolution of problems.

3. *Difficulty and Ambiguity.* Some people are very compulsive and become upset if the order of their physical life is violated. Such people prefer every thing to be at its right place. This is also true to mental processes and in certain cases ability to create a new sturcture or sequence may also

be impaired because of lack of orderliness. Although orderliness provides the advantage of aesthetics and functionality, yet it is important to have an ability to cope with asymmetry. When a new method of working is initiated, it is not possible to foresee every eventuality and predict the exact outcome. Some of the things can not be simulated and have to be tested only by experience. In many situations the data collected will be hazy or imperfect and ultimate decisions will be based upon opinion and value judgments. People who excessively depend on order will find it a hindrance. Entrepreneurs do need an ability to bring order to chaos and their first requirement is "to be able to tolerate chaos".

4. *Impatience in Solving Problems.* When people face difficult problems generally they grab the first available solution and try to implement the same. People sometimes act so because of their emotional insecurity or with a view of hiding their incompetence. As a result only the most important aspect of the problem is addressed that too inefficiently by an inadequate and unimaginative solution and the rest of the problem remain unattended. This solution mostly lacks imagination, creativity, enterprise and is normally less sustainable.

The entrepreneur has to find more creative, imaginative and sustainable solutions. Thus, setting up an enterprise needs a lot of patience and an eye for details by the entrepreneur.

5. *Lack of Clear Perception.* An entrepreneur is one who can easily identify an opportunity and exploit it for commercial gain. Most people will agree that a number of times they have failed in seeing an opportunity or an obvious solution to a problem. When the opportunity is exploited by others, they realise how their perception was based in some way or the other. Normally one is swayed by irrational prejudice and try to impose one's preconceived ideas as a solution. This behaviour is a major barrier to entrepreneurship.

❋❋❋

4

QUALITIES OF ENTREPRENEURS

The term 'competence' refers to person's underlying characteristics leading to his/her superior performance. It is a good combination of various qualities and traits required to perform the job effectively. Entrepreneurs who possess the necessary competencies succeed while those deficient in these qualities fail in their ventures.

Common people believe that entrepreneurs are born not made, business family background is essential to success for entrepreneurs. Other people, believe that entrepreneurs are made not born. According to some people, persons with proper knowledge and skills acquired through education and experience can become successful entrepreneurs. Thus to resolve the controversy on what are the traits of a successful entrepreneurs, the Entrepreneurship Development Institute of India (EDI), Ahmedabad, conducted a research study of entrepreneurs. This study has identified the following entrepreneurial competencies:

1. *Initiation.* Given the demand of the situation, the entrepreneur takes initiation to start an industry.
2. *Watching for Opportunities.* He, like a watchdog, looks for favourable business opportunity and takes necessary action accordingly.

3. *Persistence.* Follows the saying 'try and try again, you will succeed at last'. He is always tenacious to make extreme effort to get rid of the obstacles coming in the way of reaching the ultimate goal.

4. *Work Planning.* Frames realistic business plans and follows them rigorously to achieve the objectives, by minimum cost.

5. *Information Seeker.* He is ready to learn from the experience of others and enriches his business information to help him reach the goal.

6. *Commitment to Work.* Provides utmost priority to accomplish the work.

7. *Efficiency Lover.* Lover one who tries to do things at a faster pace at the minimum cost.

8. *Quality Conscious.* Always puts effort to excel better than the existing standards of performance.

9. *Self-confidence.* A strong believer in his strengths and weakness, knows his capabilities.

10. *Concern for Employees.* Keep concern and takes proper action to improve the welfare of the employees working in the enterprise.

11. *Efficient Monitoring.* Personally supervises the work to ensure that the work is accomplished according to the standards set forth without much variation.

12. *Assertiveness.* Able to assert his issues, whatsoever these might be, in the interest of enterprise.

13. *Persuasion.* Succeeds in persuading others to do what he wants.

Several other research studies have tried to identify the qualities and traits of successful entrepreneurs. In a study of entrepreneurial development, in Madras (Now Tamil Nadu) city of India, James J. Berna has stressed the following qualities of a good entrepreneur:

1. He is an enterprising individual. He is energetic, hard working, resourceful, very alert to new opportunities, able enough to adapt to changing conditions with, ease and always willing to undertake risk involved in change.
2. He is also interested in expanding the scale of his operations by way of ploughing back his profits and earnings.
3. He well visualises the likely changes and is ready to adapt them and when the changes take place.
4. He welcomes advanced technology and is interested in improving and upgrading the quality of his product or service.

B.C. Tandon has listed the four major qualities of a successful entrepreneur:

1. A successful entrepreneur should have capacity to bear risk involved in the business.
2. He should possess the required technical knowledge and should be ready to adapt to change, as and when needed.
3. An entrepreneur should also have ability to organize and manage the various factors of production to the best of his enterprise. For this, he requires high and relevant knowledge of management theory.
4. The entrepreneur should also have ability to marshal the resources this command in the best possible manner for achieving his ultimate business objectives.

According to McClelland, the successful entrepreneurs are characterised by three qualities:

1. He is endowed with an unusual creativeness.
2. He has also a strong need for achievement.
3. He is enriched by high propensity.

In nutshell the following are the qualities of a successful entrepreneurs:

1. Capacity and willingness to assume risk and uncertainties.
2. Willingness to hard work and be always tenacious about new changes.
3. Vision and foresightedness.
4. Creative and imaginative thinking.
5. Total commitment, determination and perseverance about all possible dangers.
6. High degree of ambition for future growth.
7. Innovativeness and willingness to adapt to new challenges.
8. Ability to marshall resources, if need so arise.

Role or Functions of an Entrepreneur

A successful entrepreneur recognises the commercial potential of a product or service, designs operating policies in marketing, production, product development and the organizational structure. He carries out the whole set of activities of the business. He has a high capacity for taking calculated risks and has faith in his own capabilities.

The functions of an entrepreneur are:

1. Deciding the project
2. Risk-taking
3. Innovation
4. Raising finance
5. Planning production
6. Managing enterprise
7. Earning profits

In reality an entrepreneur has to carry out a combination of these in keeping with time and environment. The entrepreneur has to react to new ideas, demands and exploit the opportunities, and thereby contributes to technical progress. He is thus a nucleus of high growth of the enterprise.

An entrepreneur is expected to perform the following role or functions:

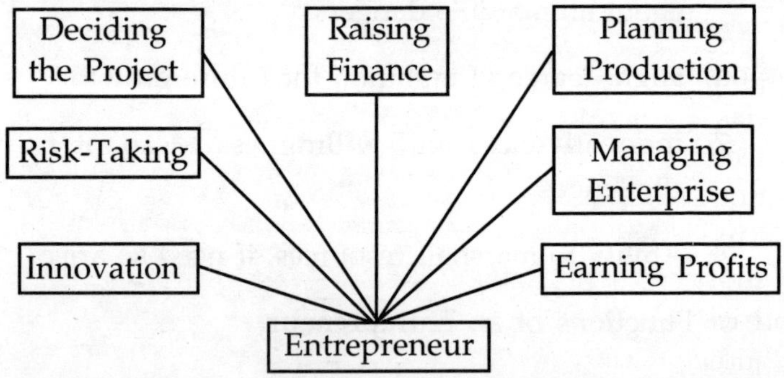

In principle, the entrepreneur could be a planner in a socialist economy or even a priest or king in a traditional society. In practice, entrepreneurship is closely identified with private enterprise in a market economy.

In nut shell he is a person who performs many useful functions, he undertakes a venture, assumes risk and earns profit. He is the man having a strong motivation to achieve success. He is self-confident in his entrepreneurial abilities. He exploits opportunities wherever and whenever they arise.

The entrepreneur can identify opportunities to start a business either as a manufacturer or as a distributor, for entrepreneurship exists in every field of economic endeavour. Manufacturing activities require a relatively high capital investment and a greater degree of entrepreneurial abilities than distribution activities. Entrepreneurship has also been developed in the trading sector. Britain, for example, has developed trading entrepreneurship while Germany and Japan have developed industrial entrepreneurship. A manufacturing entrepreneur demonstrates his entrepreneurial talents by bringing out one products while a trading entrepreneur performs his entrepreneurial functions in creating demand for the business in which he deals.

The following are the specific functions after studying the various thoughts of different economic, social and political environment These are as:

1. *Risk Bearing Capacity.* The entrepreneur assumes all possible risks of business. A business risk also involves the risk due to the possibility of changes in the tastes of consumers, techniques of production and new inventions. Such risks are not insurable. The entrepreneur has to bear the loss himself. Thus, risk-bearing or uncertainty bearing still remains the most important function of an entrepreneur. An entrepreneur tries to reduce the uncertainties by his initiative, skill and his judicious approach.

2. *Decisions-Making.* The entrepreneur has to decide to the nature and type of goods to be produced. He enters the particular industry which offers him the best prospects and products and produces whatever commodities he thinks will pay him the most and employs those methods of production which seem to him the most profitable. He effects suitable

changes in the size of the business, its location, techniques of production and does everything that is needed for the development of his business.

3. *Managerial Functions.* He formulates production plans, arranges finance, purchases raw materials, provides production facilities, organizes sales and assumes the task of personal management. In a large establishment, these management functions are delegated to the paid managerial personnel.

4. *Function of Innovation.* An important function of an entrepreneur is "innovation". He conceives that idea for the improvement in the quality of production line. He considers the economic viability and technological feasibility.

5. *Addition in Per Capita Income.* Entrepreneurs locate and exploit opportunities, convert the latent and idle resources like land, labour and capital into national income and wealth in the form of goods and services. They help to increase Net National Product and per capita income in the country, which are important yardsticks for measuring economic growth.

6. *Capital Formation.* Entrepreneurs mobilise the idle savings of the public through the issues of industrial securities. Investment of public savings in industry results in productive utilisation of national resources. Rate of capital formation increases which is essential for rapid economic growth.

7. *Creation of Employment.* Entrepreneurs generate employment both directly and indirectly. Directly, self-employment as an entrepreneur offers the best way for independent and honourable life. Indirectly, by setting up large and small scale business units they offer jobs to millions.

8. *Improvement in Living Standards.* Entrepreneurs setup industries which remove scarcity of essential commodities and introduce new products. Production of goods on mass scale and manufacture of handicrafts, etc. in the small scale

sector help to improve the standard of life of a common man. These offer goods at lower costs and increase variety in consumption.

9. *Economic—Self-Reliance.* Entrepreneurship is essential for national self-reliance. Industrialists help to manufacture indigenous substitutes of hitherto imported products thereby reducing dependence on foreign countries. Businessmen also export goods and services on a large scale and thereby earn the scarce foreign exchange for the country.

10. *Balanced Regional Development.* Entrepreneurs in the public and private sectors help to remove regional disparities in economic development. They set up industries in backward areas to avail of the various concessions and subsidies offered by the Central and State Governments. Public sector steel plants, and private sector industries by Modis, Tatas, Birlas and others have put the hitherto unknown places on the international map.

Factors Influencing Entrepreneurship

Peter Heydemann, the Science Counsellor in the US Embassy, is very much impressed with the role the small business play in the process of innovation in the US economy. He explained how "incubators" are used successfully in the United States to encourage small entrepreneurs.

The problem is how best to help small entrepreneurs translate the results of laboratory research into marketable products to transform a new scientific concept into a commercial product. Simply put, "incubators" are very basic facilities offering shad secretarial services, space for conducting a retail or manufacturing business, and a few simple machine tools. But, and this is very important, incubators offer advice and consolation on subjects with which the most budding entrepreneurs are unfamiliar; business and finance planning, market development, government regulations. Incubators have indeed greatly helped small manufacturers to develop new products. Recent studies show that such enterprises are the main source of innovation in the US industry.

The idea of incubators of technology is relatively new, "five or six years old", says Heydmann. This is because untit recently it was felt that the US industry would forever remain in the forefront, without any competition. But things changed rapidly. So, realising that "the 600 plus national laboratories could not possibly service all the one-and-a-half million or so small entrepreneurs," individua! American states took it upon themselves to help local industry through their technology support and development organizations.

Incubators are very often attached to state university systems as universities have much of the technical and non-technical information that needs to be fed to the entrepreneurs. Moreover, state universities have increasingly come to believe that apart from their traditional role, they must also promote industrial activity in their areas of operation.

State authorities in turn help by enabling businessmen cut through red tape, provide low-interest loans to develop prototypes, undertake market research and generally assist in bringing a new product to the consumer. "Some notion of the magnitude of this support can be had from the fact that last year alone, the federal and state governments together spent more than $2,000 million in encouraging small business." Many private sector companies also provide incubator facilities, though at a comparatively higher cost.

Another important aspect of incubators is that experts do not make any business decisions for their clients. They only provide guidelines and advice on product development; engineering, pilot production and in identifying markets.

Among the businesses in which incubators are making a significant contribution, says Heydemann, "are light manufacturing in mature technologies, retail and wholesale trade, and finally research and development in emerging technologies."

The success rate of incubators has been salutary in the number of new jobs created, the enlarged tax base for state revenues and in the export of manufactures. In short, incubators are bringing new vigor and vitality to America's industrial renaissance and are once more giving the country a competitive edge.

Problems the Entrepreneurship Concept

The task before the national leadership today is to industrialize a predominantly agricultural society, where capital is scarce and labour is plentiful. The modern industry implies a style and a method of work which are quite at variance with the traditional culture and modes of social behaviour in the underdeveloped countries. So, the whole structure of society has to undergo a considerable structural and institutional change commensurate with the needs of the situation.

The gap between the indigenous arts and even the improved crafts, on the one hand, and the imported and also the indigenous technology, on the other, is wide enough and is further widening day after day with the explosion of innovative research. Furthermore, the economy has been historically and unavoidably polarised between a few mighty industrial centres and the far-flung rural areas. With all the progress during the two decades and a half, the national economy is beset with all kinds of shortages and scarcities of inputs, most vital to entrepreneurs, when they launch their small or tiny units. Besides, they have; at times, to contend and compete with the well established small, medium or large industrial units in the same lines of production. Newly emerging industries, particularly of the first-generation entrepreneurs, even in the underdeveloped economies are slowly but certainly tending to become high investment.

Industries and the entrepreneurs have to battle against formidable force of hostile elements, such as:

(i) erratic shortages of raw materials,

(ii) flourishing black market,

(iii) rigged up prices by monopolists,

(iv) administrate maldistribution,

(v) gaps between official promise and performance,

(vi) inefficiency of industrial management,

(vii) irresponsible attitude to work,

(viii) rising cost of capital and credit,

(ix) deficient and arrogant institutional banking,

(x) inadequacy of common services,

(xi) primitive wholesale and retail trade outlets and others. New entrepreneurship in India has to be cradled in this environment.

The present stage of entrepreneurship development programmes as a factor contributing to the industrialisation of backward and other areas needs a proper direction and organization for making it more effective and purposeful. The contribution of entrepreneurship development programmes is very uneven among different regions and definite programmes need to be chalked out to bring about some degree of uniformity and upgradation. Before these problems are tackled, some important issues need immediate attention for example:

(i) structure and composition of entrepreneurship development programmes;

(ii) areas of operations;

(iii) fixing of priorities;

(iv) follow-up;

(v) spatial dispersal of the entrepreneurship development programmes;

(vi) training of trainees;

(vii) financing pattern.

There are some of the operational problems experience in the course of implementing the entrepreneurship development programmes are as:

1. Past experience has shown that the supporting agencies organization either tend to be slipshod in the first phase or are less interested in the third phase which means that the programme fails to tap the entrepreneurial potential of the area or the trained entrepreneurs do not receive the support and counselling which they need most.

2. Most of the existing support organization meant for maintenance operations are not for innovative functions. There is also an element of cynicism. A reorientation in the attitude of supporting organization is called for.

3. Poor investment on the part of institutions as also trainees and wrong selection of target groups contributed largely to the failure of the number of entrepreneurship development programmes.

4. It is also said that there is an indecent inability to identify the needs of institutions and differences of opinion prevailed amongst the practitioners and also amongst the trainees.

5. Experience reveal that entrepreneurial failures are mostly due to incompetence and poor management.

6. It is also stated that there is a low institutional commitment for local support to the entrepreneurs. There is also a very low level of local support to enterpreneurs. Thus, to cover-up the above problems arise the need of entre-preneural management.

7. It is also stated that there is ill-planned training methodology, inconsistency in the programme design, its content, sequence and theme and the focus of the programme is not clear.

8. Non-availability of various inputs, *i.e.*, raw materials, power etc., and infrastructure support combined with poor follow-up by the primary monetary institutions resulted in the failure of the entrepreneurship development programmes.

9. Tanning institutions do not have much concern for the objective identification and selection of entrepreneurs and the follow-up after training.

10. Some of the institutions are still debating whether to have a proper identification and selection of entrepreneurs for preparing successful entrepreneurs.

11. A majority of institutions engaged in the entrepreneurship development programmes are themselves not convinced of what they are doing as the task is delegated by the government. As a result the social objective aimed at is not achieved.

12. Those involved in and concerned with the selection and follow-up activities have either limited manpower support or a narrow linkage with other support agencies.

13. It is also said that there is no standard curricula even in terms of broad module being adopted by interventions.

14. It has also been realized that absence of an appropriate industrial and commercial climate coupled with lack of information and access to relevant technology has acted as a great handicap.

15. Mechanical implementation of entrepreneurship development programmes, as it is happening in many cases, will not solve the problems. The mechanical approach may help them (entrepreneurs) to initiate the entrepreneurial development activity but they may not be able to manage it and expand it successfully.

16. Perpetual ambiguity in the objectives of entrepreneurship development programmes seems to have percolated to the grassroots level with significant deterioration in terms of content and interest.

5

ENTREPRENEURIAL DEVELOPMENT IN INDIA

Entrepreneurial development is an organized and systematic development. It is now regarded as a tool of industrialisation and a solution to unemployment problem. The objective of entrepreneurial development is to motivate a person for entrepreneurial career and to make him capable of perceiving and exploiting successfully opportunities for entetprises. One trained entrepreneur can guide others on how to start their own enterprise and approach various institutions. In fact trained entrepreneurs become catalysts of developing industry and economic progress.

Entrepreneurial Development Programme (EDP) may be defined as "a programme designed to help an individual in strengthening his entrepreneurial motive and in acquiring skills and capabilities necessary for playing his entrepreneurial role effectively.

The main objectives of an entrepreneurial development programme are as follows:

1. To identify and train potential entrepreneurs for covering risk and uncertanties.
2. To impart basic managerial understanding to face new challenges.
3. To provide post-training assistance for future growth.

4. To develop necessary knowledge and skills among the participants.

Mainly there are three approaches used for entrepreneurial development.

(i) Product-Oriented Approach. It focused on the project and its policies which are framed in the beginning.

(ii) Government Contribution. As Government of India laid main emphasis on large and heavy industries such as Hindustan Steel, and BHEL.

(iii) Industrial Policy 1956. Which focus the need of growth of small scale industries and balance regional development.

Government gave from time to time several concessions, yet the desired result are not obtained the main reasons of failure are:

- Lack of proper integration between person, project and policy was the main cause of failure. Attempts were made to strengthen the project. District Industries Centres were made stronger to identify projects at the district level. Small Industries Service Institutes, Technical Consultancy Organization, State Financial Corporations and other agencies started counselling the viable projects suitable to a particular place. No special attempt was made to develop the person perhaps due to the assumption that everyone can become an entrepreneur.

- SIET Institute, Hyderabad, for the first time attempted to develop person as entrepreneur through structural training. The main purpose of such entrepreneurial development programme is to widen the base of entrepreneurship by developing achievement motivation and entrepreneurial skills among the less privileged sections of society.

Need for Training and Development

One of the factors contributing to the success of this training intervention in entrepreneurship developments that it is based on experiences. In entrepreneurship training, learning by discovery is usually preferred. Here, one is able to learn from one's actions and behaviour in training, learring by discovery is usually preferred. Here, one is able to learn from one's action and behaviour in training.

Designing an Entrepreneurship Training Programme. As mentioned earlier, designing the training programme involves setting training objectives, developing the course content and choosing appropriate training methods.

The programme design is prescribed by the training needs of the target clientele. These objectives should be stated clearly, be trainee-centered, employ practically and be concerned with ends rather than means. When objectives are set, the course content can be developed. The elements of content are knowledge, habits, skills and control of emotion. The material to be included should be accorded priority according to the goal to be achieved.

Gateways into the Curriculum

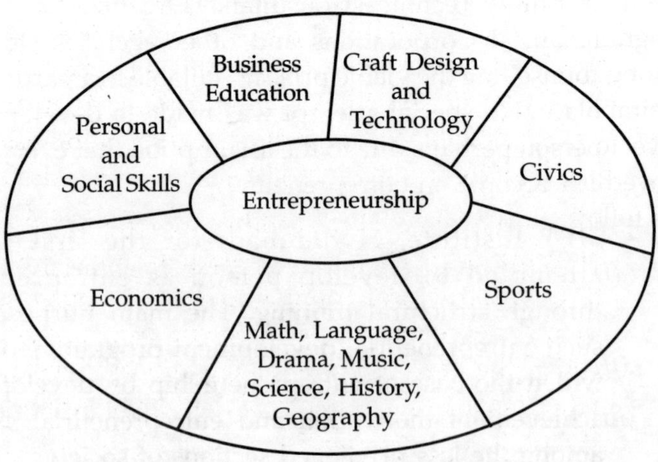

Phases or Approach of Entrepreneurial Development Programme (EDP). In general there are three phases for Entrepreneurial Development Programme namely as:

(1) *Initial or Pre-training Phase.* Here the activities relating to the training programme which covers the identification and selection of potential entrepreneurs and provide initial motivation to entrepreneurs, thus:

(a) Creation of infrastructure for training.

(b) Preparation of training syllabus.

(c) Tie up of guest faculty.

(d) Arrangement for inauguration of the programme.

(e) Formation of selection committee.

(f) Designing tools and techniques for selecting the trainees.

(g) Publicity campaign for the programme.

(h) Development of application form.

(i) Pre-potential survey of environmental opportunities.

(2) *Training or Development Phase.* In this phase the training programme is implemented to develop motivation and skills among the participants. The objective of this phase is to bring desirable changes in the behaviour of the trainees. The trainers have to judge how much, and how far the tradinees have moved in their entrepreneurial pursuits. A trainer should see the following changes in the behaviour of participants.

(i) Is there any change in his entrepreneurial outlook, role and skill?

(ii) How should be behave like an entrepreneur?

(iii) What kind of entrepreneurial behaviour does the trainee lack?

(iv) Is he skilful in choosing the right project, mobilising the right resources at the right time?

(v) Does he possess the knowledge of technology, resources and other related entrepreneurial knowledge?

(3) *Post-training or Follow-up Phase.* This phase involves assessment to judge how far the objectives of the programme have been achieved. Monitoring and follow up reveals drawbacks in the earlier phases and suggests guidelines for framing the future policy. In this phase infrastructural support, counselling and assistance in establishing new enterprise and in developing the existing units can also be reviewed.

Meaning of Development

Economic development has been a focal point right from the days of Adam Smith, Ricardo, Mill, Schumpter and other noted economists. Adam Smith did not assign any significance to entrepreneurial role in his monumental work 'An Inquiry into the Nature and Causes of the Wealth of Nations' published in 1776.

Ricardo identified machinery, capital, and labour as three important factors of production. According to Ricardo, profit leads to saving of wealth, which ultimately goes to capital formation and leads to economic development. According to Lewis the proximate ways of economic development are: the effort to economise, the increase of knowledge and its application to production and increasing the amount of capital or other resources per head. Since economic development is closely associated with 'human endowments', social attitudes, political conditions and historical accidents, only economic requirements for development are not enough.

The thinking of the economists during 1950s and early 1960s focused mainly on the concept of 'stages of economic growth' in which the process of development was viewed as a series of successive stages through which all countries must pass. It was primarily an economic theory of development in which the right quantity and mixture of saving, investment, and foreign aid were all that was necessary to enable developing nations to proceed along an economic growth path that historically had been followed by the more developed countries. Development thus became synonymous with rapid, aggregate economic growth. This linear stages approach has now been replaced to a great extent by two competing economic schools of thought. The first, the 'neoclassical structural change models', uses modern economic theory and statistical analysis in an attempt to portray the internal process of structural change that a 'typical' developing country must undergo if it is to succeed in generating and sustaining a process of rapid economic growth. The second, the 'international dependence paradigms', is more radical and political in orientation. It views under-development in terms of international and domestic power relationships, institutional and structural economic rigidities, and the resulting proliferation of dual economies and dual societies both within and among the nations of the world. Dependence theories tend to emphasise external and internal institutional and political constraints on economic development. Emphasis is placed on the need for major new policies to eradicate poverty, to provide more diversified employment opportunities, and to reduce income inequalities. These and other egalitarian objectives are to be achieved within the context of a growth economy, but economic growth *per se* is not given the exalted status accorded to it by the linear stages and the structural change models.

Objectives of Development

Development is both a physical reality and a state of mind in which society has, through some combination of social, economic, and institutional processes, secured the means for obtaining a better life. For better life, development in all societies must have at least the following three objectives:

1. To increase the availability and widen the distribution of basic life-sustaining goods such as food, shelter, health and protection.
2. To raise levels of living including, in addition to higher incomes, the provision of more jobs, better education, and greater attention to cultural and humanist values, all of which will serve not only to enhance material well-being but also to generate greater individual and national self-esteem.
3. To expand the range of economic and social choices available to individuals and nations by freeing them from servitude and dependence not only in relation to other people and nation-states but also to the forces of ignorance and human misery.

Index of Development

A common economic index of development has been the use of rates of growth of per capita Gross National Product (GNP) to take into account the ability of a nation to expand its output at a rate faster than the growth rate of its population. Levels and rates of growth of 'real' per capita GNP are normally used to measure in a broad sense the overall economic well-being of a population that is, how much of real goods and services are available tor consumption and investment for the average citizen. Whether or not a country has undergone development can also be gauged by seeking answer to the following questions:

— Have general levels of living within a nation risen to the point that there has been a lessening of absolute poverty (*i.e.,* deprivation of life-sustaining goods) and of inequality in income distribution, as well as improvements in the level of employment and the nature and quality of education, health, and other social and cultural services?

— Has economic progress enhanced individual and group esteem both internally *vis-a-vis* one another and externally *vis-a-vis* other nations and regions?

— Finally, has economic progress expanded the range of human choice and freed people from external dependence and internal servitude to other men and institutions, rather than merely substituting one form of dependence (*e.g.*, economic) for another (*e.g.*, cultural)?

Linkage between Entrepreneurship and Economic Development

Development brings changes in economic life as are not forced upon it from without but arise by its own initiative, from within. Economic development is not a phenomenon to be explained economically, but that the economy, in itself without development is dragged along by the changes in the surrounding world. Growth of an economy in terms of wealth which its population possess should not be designated as a process of development. For it calls forth no qualitatively new phenomena, but only process of adaptation of the same kind as the change in the natural data.

Every concrete process of development finally rests upon preceding development. Ever process of development creates the pre-requisites for the following. Thereby the form of the latter is altered and things will turnout differently from what they would have been if every concrete phase of development had been completed first to create its own conditions. Development according to Schumpeter is a distinct phenomenon, entirely foreign to what may be observed in the circular flow or in the tendency towards equilibrium. It is spontaneous and discontinuous change in the channels of the flow, disturbance of equilibrium, which forever alters and displaces the equilibrium state previously existing.

In real life, development of industrial and commercial activities and spontaneous and discontinuous changes in consumer's taste disturb centre of equilibrium. Businessman in the process of coping with such disequilibrium identifies opportunities for himself. It is however, the producer who as a rule initiates economic change, and consumers are educated by him if necessary; they are as it were, taught to want new things or things which differ in some respect or other from those which they have been in the habit of using. The producer combines material and forces so as to meet the wants of consumers.

According to J.B. Say the entrepreneur's function is to combine the productive factors to bring them together. Carrying out of new combination of productive factors is called 'enterprise' which in fact is fundamental phenomenon of economic development. The individual whose function is to carry them out is what we call 'entrepreneur'.

The entire chance and development of the civilization to a large extent is the result of trade, commerce and industrialisation. In this development the human resource in general and entrepreneur in particular plays a pivotal role. McClelland his rightly hypothesised that the need for achievement in individuals, *i.e.,* the entrepreneurial potential is the psychological factor which engenders economic growth and decline. The sense of high need achievement and motivation introduced by entrepreneurs bring about the required necessities in a class of society which transform the perception of the economic thinking, which is necessary to bring about the economic development.

In the words of Rostow, 'the behaviour pattern of people relevant for economic development can be summed up in six propensities': the propensity to develop fundamental science to apply science to economic ends to accept the possibilities of innovation to seek material advance to consume and to have children.

Kuznets highlighted the role of human resources when he said, the major capital development is the body of knowledge amassed from tested findings and discoveries of empirical science, and the capacity and training of its population to use this knowledge effectively.

Tinbergin has suggested five human qualities which are conducive to economic development:

— an interest in material well-being;

— an interest in techniques, and in innovation;

— an ability to look ahead, and a willingness to take risks; perseverance; and

— an ability to collaborate with other people and to observe certain rules.

According to him presence of these qualities in individuals help a nation achieve faster economic development.

Till the beginning of industrial revolution entrepreneurship of high order was not much needed. However, peasants, artisans, feudal lords and capitalists used to perform these low order entrepreneurial functions. Advances in science and technology coupled with awareness of the economic backwardness have resulted in changed role of entrepreneur in the developing countries. In the present context, it is the Schumpeterian innovative entrepreneur who puts the science and technology in economic use. Schumpeterian innovative entrepreneurs are the key to rapid industrialisation and thereby economic development.

According to Kilby, the entrepreneur performs following four major tasks:

(i) Exchange relationship,

(ii) Practical administration,

(iii) Management control, and

(iv) Technology.

These four tasks consists of:

(i) Exchange Relationship:

(a) Perceiving opportunities in market.

(b) Gaining command over scarce resources.

(c) Purchasing inputs.

(d) Marketing of products and responding to competition.

(ii) Practical Administration:

(a) Dealing with public bureaucracy.

(b) Management of human relations within the venture.

(c) Management of customer and supplier relations.

(iii) Management Control:

(a) Financial Management.

(b) Production Management.

(iv) Technology:

(a) Acquiring and overseeing assembling of the factory.

(b) Industrial engineering.

(c) Upgrading process and product quality.

(d) Introduction of new production techniques and products.

All above fields of activities involve entrepreneur in decision-making under conditions of uncertainty. Thus, entrepreneur within Kilby's proposed framework would involve *(i)* a determination of the types and degrees of uncertainty confronting the performance of a particular operation, and *(ii)* the ability to make the appropriate decisions, necessarily for the goal attainment.

Kilby concludes, entrepreneurial performance in those roles involving 'exchange relationships' and 'practical administration' is vigorous and effective. On the other hand, entrepreneurs typically do not apply themselves with equal intensity or skill to their tasks in the realms of management control and technology. Deficiencies in these latter areas represent in many instances the operational bottlenecks to indigenous industrial development.

In the recent decades the role of an entrepreneur has been considered of very great significance in accelerating the pace of growth and economic development in both the developed and underdeveloped countries. The present day developed countries like America, England, Germany, Japan, etc. owe much of their economic development to enterprising people of their respective countries. Developing and underdeveloped countries having seen the history of economic development in developed countries are now conscious of the significance of entrepreneurship for economic development. There is growing realization that both quantity and quality of entrepreneurs are of utmost significance for achieving the goal of economic development. Active and enthusiastic entrepreneurs can fully exploit the potentialities of a country's available resources like labour, technology, and capital.

Some of the noted economists have described the role of entrepreneur in economic development in different words.

Schumpeter considers introducing innovation as the most significant contribution of entrepreneur in economic development. Parsons and Smelser describe entrepreneur as one of the two necessary conditions for economic development, the other being the increased input of capital. Harginson considers entrepreneur among the prime movers of innovation and Sayigh simply describes entrepreneurship as a necessary dynamic force.

Underdeveloped economies usually suffer from paucity of funds, lack of skilled labour and no existence of a minimum social and economic overheads. Market environment in such economies is less conducive to the emergence of innovative entrepreneurs. In such countries non-innovative entrepreneur, namely, imitators, fabian and drone are noticed to a large extent. In absence of industrial background and well developed institutional support entrepreneurs in such economies try to copy innovations introduced by innovative entrepreneurs in developed countries. Enterprising people possessing high need for achievement in such areas would be noticed not being satisfied with present status that they have in the society. They would, therefore, venture into some new type of enterprises, which usually are imitative in nature. Entrepreneurs play pivotal role in social-economic development and industrialization of a country needs no further emphasis. Entrepreneurship need not simply be confined to industry, trade and commerce, in fact, pace of development would be far greater when people in general in all walks of life and in all work situations start reflecting entrepreneurial behaviour. Developing economies need greater number of people possessing entrepreneurial qualities and capable of taking decisions under conditions of uncertainties. It is this class of human resource which has the potential of transforming their underdeveloped economies into developed economies.

Defining Entrepreneur

Entrepreneurship started catching up in 1980s just as professionalism in management caught up during 1970s. However, confusion still prevails as to what exactly we mean by the term entrepreneur. An attempt therefore, has been made here to define entrepreneur.

There is generally no accepted definition or model of what the entrepreneur is or does. Much of the literature on entrepreneur is fragmented and highly controversial. In the past decade, a number of trends have emerged which distinguish between individual entrepreneurship and corporate entrepreneurship and entrepreneurs and small business owners. The literature abounds with criteria ranging from creativity, innovation, risk taking, high need achievement, etc. to personal traits such as appearance and style. Models of the entrepreneurial leader are almost as plentiful as the number of authors who write about them.

The French Economist Cantillon, the first to introduce the term entrepreneur, defined him as an agent who purchased the means of production for combination into marketable products. Furthermore, at the moment of the factor purchases, the entrepreneur was unaware of the eventual price which he would receive for his product.

In the early 16th century France, the term entrepreneur was used for army leader. It was applied to business for the first time in 18th century, to designate a dealer who buys and sells goods at uncertain prices.

Say while defining entrepreneur laid emphasis on bringing together of the factors of production and the provision of continuing management, as well as risk-bearing.

Schumpeter played with the world innovation and emphasized innovation as the function of an entrepreneur.

Schumpeter's entrepreneur is highly specialised concern. The entrepreneur in Schumpeters theory sees the potentiality, profitable opportunities and exploit them. The entrepreneurs motivation for profit is based not merely on his desire to raise consumption standard, but also on such non-hedonistic goals as the desire to find a private dynasty. The will to conquer in the competitive battle and the job of creating, *i.e.*, he tries to maximize his profits by innovations. His unique characteristic is that he gets satisfaction from using his capabilities in attacking problems. According to Schumpeter innovation may occur in the following form:

— Introduction of new goods;

— the use of new method of production;

— the opening of a new market;

— the conquest of a new source of supply of raw materials; and

— the reorganization of any industry.

During early 20th century, Dewing equated entrepreneur with business promoter and viewed the promoter as one who transformed ideas into a profitable business. In enumerating the characteristics of a successful entrepreneur, Dewing wrote of the qualities of imagination, initiative, judgement and restraint.

Casson in his work, having considered both functional definition and an indicative definition describes 'an entrepreneur as someone who specialises in taking judgemental decisions about the co-ordination of scarce resources'.

ILO describes 'entrepreneurs are people who have the ability to see and evaluate business opportunities; together the necessary resources to take advantage of them and to initiate appropriate action to ensure success'.

In Danhof's analysis an entrepreneur "is primarily concerned with changes in the formula of production over which he has full control...He devotes correspondingly little time to the carrying out of a specific formula." Danhof divides the functions of the entrepreneur into three major roles: obtaining relevant information, evaluating the information with regard to profit....and setting the operation in motion. Major emphasis in Danhof's definition is decision-making, or judgment under alternative choices.

Cunningham and Lischerson in their recent work have described six possible schools of thought on entrepreneurship. The first school of thought, *i.e.*, 'Great Person School' says that an entrepreneur is born with an intuitive ability—a sixth sense and this sense helps him in start up stage. The second school of thought, *i.e.* 'Psychological Characteristics School' explains that entrepreneurs have unique values attitudes, and needs which drive them and help them especially in start-up stage. The third school, *i.e.* 'Classical School of Thought' says that central characteristic of entrepreneurial behavioural is innovation. This characteristic helps the entrepreneur much in start-up and early growth. 'Management School' is the fourth school of thought and it says entrepreneurs are organizers of economic venture and they organize, own, manage and assume its risk. Such functional orientation helps them in early growth and maturity. The fifty school of thought is the 'Leadership School'. According to this school entrepreneurs are leaders of people and they have the ability to adopt their style to the needs of people. Such leadership personality suits them most during early growth and maturity situations. 'Entrepreneurship School' is the sixth school of thought. Entrepreneurship is the act of developing independent units to create, market and expand services within the organization. Entrepreneurship is needed by an entrepreneur during the situation of maturity and change.

Whatever be the definition, across the world entrepreneurs have been considered instrumental in initiating and sustaining socio-economic development. There are evidences to believe that countries which have proportionately higher percentage of entrepreneurs in their population have developed much faster as compared to countries which have lesser percentage of them in the society, discover new sources of supply of materials and markets and they establish new and more effective forms of organizations. Entrepreneurs perceive new opportunities and seize them with super normal will power and energy, essential to overcome the resistance that social environment offers.

***

6

SOCIAL RESPONSIBILITIES AND OBLIGATIONS

An entrepreneur is very much linked with society. Since any venture owes its existence to society, it has to function under the overall control and discipline of the society. Any business, which is injurious to any segment of the society, can neither be tolerated nor allowed to continue. Every enterprise is required to perform and satisfy certain obligations which it owes to the society and the performance of which is essential for its own survival and the well-being of the society. It is the obligation of an enterprise which it owes to the different segments of the society that determine its objectives. Besides earning profit, an entrepreneur has to satisfy the requirements of various other groups of people. According to H.R. Brown, an entrepreneur, today, has an obligation to pursue those policies, to make those decisions or to follow those lines of action which are desirable, in terms of the objectives and values of the society. The entrepreneur, therefore, has to include his social obligations and social values as inputs into the decision and action process, along with organizational, economic, technological and other relevant values and variables.

"In the real sense, the assumption of social responsibilities implies recognition and understanding of the aspirations of a society and determination to contribute to its achievement." "Social responsibility is the personal obligation of everyone as he acts for his own interests, to assume that the rights and legitimate interests of all others are not impugned."

—*Koontz O'Donnell*

Conceptually, social responsibility may be taken to mean 'intelligent and objective concern for the welfare of the society.' It may involve both internal and external actions. Justice to employees along with creating more employment opportunities are both the facts of social responsibility. It may also involve postponement of short-term profits for earning long-term profits.

Social Responsibilities of the Modern Entrepreneur

An enterprise must earn profits for its own survival, for expansion, for bearing the risks and finally for the prestige of its management. But profit cannot be the sole objective of the entrepreneur. It is a means and not an end. No enterprise can last long unless along with earning profits, it continues to fulfil its obligations to the society. The ultimate objective of every enterprise has to be the good of the people. Business must be run by the people through the people and for the people.

Big entrepreneurs, in the past, have been engaging themselves in and spending a part of their profits on philanthropic activities such as opening of schools, hospitals, temples, etc. But, today, entrepreneurs are usually charged of exploiting the share-holders, consumers and workers, deceiving the Government and neglecting social interest. All this is partly because of the way the profits are earned by the entrepreneur and partly because of the way they consume or spend those profits. Consciousness has grown and the public outlook is fast changing. A company is no longer be only an engine for profiteering, capital creation and business expansion. Today, it is a vital national social and economic institution called upon to assume larger responsibilities. People, now-a-days, expect entrepreneurs only to act as trustees of national wealth. They should increase the wealth of the nation and draw out of it for their own consumption only that portion which is equivalent to what is ordinarily available to the common man of this country. They must share their prosperity with the other members of the society. They must allow the workers to participate both in the profits as well as in the management of the enterprise. They must stop profiteering at the cost of the consumers. They must give up unfair trade practices.

Entrepreneurs sometimes do not appreciate their obligations towards the society. They consider business to be primarily an economic system exclusively meant for maximization of profits. They consider profits ony for the shareholders. They are also afraid of the fact that social obligations will increase the cost of production of the consumers, *i.e.,* 'taxation without representation'. Increasing costs of production will reduce the competitiveness of business and will put it at a disadvantage. They do not consider enterprise as a welfare organization or a social institution. They believe that a man works only for himself and not for others.

Trade unions, consumers' associations, shareholders' bodies by their actions, and the Government, by its policies, have brought about a big change in the outlook of the entrepreneur. They have begun to appreciate human relations approach and have accepted the principle of better conditions of work for better morale of the workers. In their self interest, entrepreneurs have started thinking about social responsibilities. They have started providing more details about the working of the enterprise to the shareholders, selling goods cheaper to increase their sales, improved quality of production to build-up their image, raised wages to increase the efficiency of workers, etc. There is nothing wrong in these policies so long as they result in common good.

Why should Entrepreneurs Assume Social Obligations?

Entrepreneurs, today, are forced, by a large number of factors, discussed below, to realize and honour social obligations and to tone down substantially their pure economic objectives of profit maximization. They have to recognise the importance of the contribution of the human factor in their own long-term interest. Threat of nationalization or greater State regulation of industry, growth of consumers' movement and mobilization of public opinion to improve the quality of life and the professionalization of management is compelling the entrepreneurs to fulfil their responsibilities towards the society.

1. *To Prevent Misuse of Economic Power.* Power to command national resources has been delegated to them by the society for a specific purpose, *i.e.,* to generate more wealth. They must honour social obligations along with delegated economic power.

2. *To Avoid Misuse of National Resource.* Entrepreneurs command considerable power on the resources of the country. They are obliged to use those resources for the common good of the society. Their misdeeds in squandering away those resources cannot be tolerated.

3. *To Develop Expertise.* With their knowledge and experience, a businessman must provide leadership to the society and assist it in solving its problems; there is great need for the development of technical expertise in the country.

4. *To Increase Productivity.* Long-term enlightened self-interest requires that the entrepreneur must give due importance to social obligations in order to optimise the total economic and social productivity of corporate resources under his command. An effort must be made to contain prices and overcome shortages.

5. *To Satisfy Social Needs.* Professional management is fast growing in our country. They are likely to act more in the

social interest rather than their own personal interest as they do not carry any financial stakes in the business which they are asked to manage. They are more wedded to the fulfilment of the national, social, economic objectives.

6. *To Avoid Class Conflicts.* Entrepreneurs must try to avoid class conflict in their own interest. Industrial peace is essential for the success of an enterprise. Trade unions are pressing hard for social welfare measures, for better wages, for better conditions of work, for their participation in decision-making, etc.

7. *To Cooperate with Government Policy.* The Government has adopted the policy of socialistic pattern of society in which private interest has to cooperate with the overall national interest of avoiding concentration of wealth and providing opportunities of growth to everyone.

8. *To Win Over Public Confidence.* Growing public consciousness, pressure from money-lending institutions to conform to the declared social policy of the Government and the need for the development of technical expertise in the country are certain other factors, which are making it necessary for an entrepreneur to fulfil his social obligations more vigorously and ungrudingly.

Profit Objective *Vs.* Social Objective

It is wrong to think that there is any conflict between profit objective and social obligations. It is a very important social obligation of an entrepreneur to manage the enterprise most efficiently. Profit, in enterprise, is necessary to fulfil social obligations. It is a symptom of good business health.

Profit is necessary for survival as well as for growth. It is also needed to earn prestige to innovate and introduce new ideas and techniques to assess a manager's performance and development to provide better conditions of work for the workers, etc. An enterprise suffering from losses cannot continue for long and its closure may hit different sections of the society adversely. According to Peter Drucker, the "problem of any enterprise is not maximization of profit but the achievement of sufficient profit to cover risks of economic activity and thus, to avoid loss." And therefore, the moment profits are misused either for individual satisfaction or to exploit society by establishing monopolies, hoarding of goods, acquiring political power, etc., they become a curse to the society.

The profit maximization objective of enterprises suffers from several serious shortcomings. It encourages concentration of economic power in a few hands. Those who acquire economic power also wield political power. Concentration of economic and political power in the selected few enables them to misuse it against public interest. They are able to influence Government policies to their own advantage. Irresponsible power elites perpetuate their control over industry. Family dominated managements do not allow professional managements to grow, workers' and consumers' exploitation continues unabated. The environment is polluted and the quality of life goes down.

According to Urwick, "earning profits cannot be the objective of a business any more than eating is the objective of living." The initial love of a good management should be to efficiently utilise and conserve corporate resources to produce economic wealth and bring about economic welfare. Entrepreneurs must, along with earning profits, protect the legitimate rights and interests of shareholders, workers, customers and the conununity as a whole. Nothing can be a bigger offence than to increase one's profits by evasion of taxes, by selling sub-standard or underweight goods to the consumers, by asking the workers to work under inhuman conditions, etc. No one can be allowed to earn profits by acting in a manner which is inconsistent with the social economic policies and the philosophy of the Government.

Entrepreneurs, while earning profits, cannot be negligent to the indirect adverse effects of their activities on the society such as the problem of pollution, unemployment, ill health, deteriorating working condiıions, etc.

Business must take proper care of the feelings, attitudes and the relations among the people who work for it. It should be used as an organ of growth, expansion and change in economy. It must encourage innovation and research. It must meet the needs of the community.

Business must satisfy legal requirements and continue to follow customary practices regarding its social obligations. It should adopt a long range view while it is asked to perform socially responsible actions with increasing economic power and social obligations. The enterprise must solve all those social problems for the generation for which it is responsible. Self-interest, therefore, should not supercede social interest.

The conflict between profit objective and social obligations arises only when the entrepreneur begins to act contrary to the ideology and general values of our society. No one shall object to the profits of an enterprise so long as the business continues to fulfil its social obligations.

Obligations of the Entrepreneur to the Different Segments of the Society

Business, today, has become a profession of public service and the entrepreneur has to act as a public trustee. He is required to deal with two groups of society: *(a)* insiders, *i.e.*, the shareholders or proprietors of the business and the employees therein, and *(b)* outsiders, which may include consumers, creditors, the Government and the conununity as a whole. This is not a very rigid classification because the same person may be a shareholder, creditor, an employee and a consumer of the business, all at the same time. Governments, now-a-days are also owning, financing and controlling several big businesses. In certain cases, they may be biggest consumers of the products of their own factories, such as, ammunitions.

According to Earnest Dale, "the manager sees himself as an arbiter among the many interests of 'public' affected by the business, the stockholders, the employees, the suppliers, the local community and the customers. It is his duty to divide the returns from the business equitably by providing a 'fair' return to the shareholders, 'fair' working conditions and pay for the employees or 'fair' prices to the suppliers and customers and to make the business, in general, an asset to the local community and the nation."

The most important social obligation of an entrepreneur is to reconcile and balance the various conflicting interests in the best possible manner.

1. *Owners of Business.* An entrepreneur must provide safe, fair, adequate and stable long-run rate of return and steady capital appreciation to the shareholders for their investments. It must also provide regular, accurate and adequate information about the working of the company. Maximum disclosure about the latter's progress and achievements is very much satisfying to the shareholders. It must ensure planned growth, solvency of the enterprise and optimum utilization of the resources of the enterprise.

2. *Employees.* Employees need security of job, higher wages, full employment, better conditions of work and opportunities for self-development and promotion. They want to unite and form trade unions to achieve their rights and to seek protection against high-handedness of the management. They also desire their work itself to be rewarding and to contribute something good to the society in general. Management, as a part of its social responsibilities, is expected to provide for their social security, welfare, grievances settlement machinery and sharing of excess profits.

Entrepreneurs should lose no opportunity to negotiate with the labour unions at the earliest and to create better understanding with the workmen through collective bargaining.

Management should serve as a model employer by providing stable employment, adequate wages, good and safe working conditions, job satisfaction and opportunities for self-development. Healthy trade union practices may be encouraged. Employees should be considered as partners in business since their interest in business is not very much different from the interest of the shareholders. They should be allowed to participate in the decision-making process at all levels of management.

3. *Consumers.* In the words of Henry Ford, an entrepreneur must provide "those goods and services which the society needs at a price which the society can afford to pay."

The entrepreneur is expected to provide good quality of goods to the consumers at reasonable prices. He should develop a liberal and fair attitude towards the consumers. He must maintain regular supply of high quality of products and provide all courtesies and services to the consumers.

Entrepreneurial ventures must meet the requirements of the consumers of different classes, tastes and with different purchasing power at the right time, place, price and in right quality. An entrepreneur should act as a friend and guide to the consumer. He must try to protect consumers' interest at all costs. He must guard against adulteration, poor quality, lack of service and courtesy to the consumer, misleading and dishonest advertisement, underweighing, supply of stale goods, etc. He must handle the complaints of the consumers carefully and efficiently and cooperate to the maximum extent with the consumers' associations.

4. *Suppliers.* Dealings with the suppliers should be based on integrity, impartiality and courtesy. Terms and conditions regarding delivery of goods and payment of prices must be reasonably fair. Producers may make available to the suppliers the benefits of their information and research so as to promote indigenous growth or for the improvement of the quality of their products. They can be very helpful in predicting future market trends.

5. *Competitors and Fellow Businessmen.* An entrepreneur should develop healthy inter-business relationships with fellow-entrepreneurs. He must adopt fair trade practices regarding prices, quality, terms and conditions of sale and after-sales service. The policy of under-cutting or restricted trade practices should be avoided. An entrepreneur must patronise business associations to ensure development of healthy business practices.

6. *Government.* Entrepreneurs must abide by the laws of the country in their true spirit.

They must so conduct their affairs as may cause the minimum possible social damage such as air or water pollution. They must help in the proper implementation of all social improvement policies adopted by the Government such as checking population explosion; prevention of deforestation, eradication of malaria, removal of educated unemployment.

They must cooperate with the formulation and the administration of laws. They must pay taxes honestly and promptly. They should assist the government in formulating suitable laws to govern business activities and eradicating the evil of corruption from public offices.

7. *Community.* Entrepreneurs must behave as good citizens. They should not try to encroach on the rights of their fellow beings. They should use their resources for the welfare of the society. They should try to refrain from operlent and

unneccessary display of wealth. They may provide financial and technical help to the local bodies to improve public services such as regular water supply, sewer and sanitation, education and medical facilities. They may also encourage cultural activities and promote art, music, sports, etc. They should spread know-how and encourage talent to come up. Besides improving the living conditions of people, they may encourage development of education and research. The may take up such schemes and policies which are likely to reduce costs of production or increase the efficiency of workers. They may take measures to uplift the weaker sections of the society. They may adopt villages around their industries and take steps for their all round improvement. They may provide for better health, recreation facilities, child care, uplift of the rural masses, etc. Finally, the entrepreneurs should manage their business with such competence and skill that it inspires confidence and pride in the minds of the people. They must encourage democratic institutions and assist national integration. Enterprise, on the whole, should act on the ideas of social justice without discrimination of any kind. Business must set high standards of morality and put in all efforts to minimize social damage. It must encourage democratic institutions and assist national integration. It must help in bringing about a cultural, social and economic revolution in the society and lead to the economic growth of the backward regions of the world. It must help in maintaining uniform and reasonable trade practices throughout the world. It must cause spread of knowledge in the less developed countries of the world. It must help in the preservation of international peace.

***

7

EMERGENCE OF ENTREPRENEURIAL CLASS

If one is to see the historical facts for the emergence of entrepreneurial development in India, the fact is this the advent of East India Company. This Company introduced various changes in Indian industry for example, raw materials were exported to UK and the finished goods of these raw materials imported to India. The Parsis made good use of this policy as they could maintain good relation with East India Company. The most important was shipwright Lowjee-Nushirvan, who migrated to Bombay (Now Mumbai) around 1935. He belonged to a Wadia family which gave birth to many leading ship-builders of Bombay. In 1677, Manjee Dhanjee was given a contract for building the first large gunpowder mill in Bombay for the East India Company. Besides, a Parsi foreman of a gun factory belonging to the Company established a steel industry in Bombay in 1852. On the basis of these facts, it can be stated that the East India Company made some contribution towards entrepreneurial growth in India. The Company did it deliberately for the growth of entrepreneurship in India or it was just a coincidence that people came in contact with the Company and entered the manufacturing, nothing can be said with authority.

The emergence of manufacturing entrepreneurship can be noticed in the second half of 19th century. Prior to 1850, some stray failure attempts were, indeed, made by the

Europeans to set up factories in India. In the beginning, the Paris were the founder manufacturing entrepreneurs in India, to name a few as:

> Ranchodlal Chotalal, a Nagar Brahman, was the first Indian to think of setting up the textile manufacturing on the modern factory lines in 1847, but failed. In his second attempt, he succeeded in setting up a textile mill in 1861 at Ahmedabad. The first cotton textile manufacturing unit was already setup by a Parsi-Cowasjee Nanabhoy Davar—in Bombay in 1854 followed by Nawrosjee Wadia, who opened his textile mill Bombay in 1880. The credit for the expansion of textile industries up to 1915 goes to the Parsis. Out of 96 textile mills existing in 1915, 43 per cent (41) were setup by Parsis, 24 per cent (23) by Hindus, 10 per cent (10) by Muslims and 20 per cent (22) by foreigners, *i.e.*, British citizens. Later, the Parsis invaded other fields, mainly iron and steel industry, also. Jamshedjee Tata was the first Paris entrepreneur who established the first steel industry in Jamshedpur in 1911.

The Swadeshi Movement gave a much needed boost to indigenous entrepreneurship. The second wave of entrepreneurial growth began after the First World War. The Government adopted the policy of discriminating protection. It stipulated that companies receiving protection should be registered in India with rupee capital and some Indians as directors. These measures helped the growth of manufacturing industries in the country. In 1813, the East India Company lost its monopoly. European and Indian managing agents emerged to provide venture capital and entrepreneurial talent. Partition of the country in 1947 caused some harm to the growth of entrepreneurship.

Historical development chart showing how the term is used in different period and by different authorities.

Developing of Entrepreneurship Theory and Term Entrepreneur

The word "entrepreneur" is derived from the French verb entreprendre. It means "to undertake."

In the early 16th century, the French attributed this term to people who organized and/or led military expeditions. All those people who were responsible to find new land were also called "entrepreneur".

17th century	:	person bearing risks of profits (loss) in a fixed price contract with government.
1725 : Richard Cantillon	:	person bearing risks in different from one supplying capital.
1797 : Beaudeau	:	person bearing risks, planning, supervising, organizing and owning.
1803 : Jean Baptiste Say	:	separated profits of entrepreneur from profits of capital.
1876 : Francis Walker	:	distinguished between those who supplied funds and received interest and those who received profit from managerial capabilities.
1934 : Joseph Schumpeter	:	an entrepreneur is an innovator and develops untried technology.
1938 : Haggen	:	an entrepreneur is an economic man who tries to maximize his profits by innovations.
1961 : David McClelland	:	entrepreneur is an energetic moderate risk taker.
1964 : Peter Drucker	:	entrepreneur maximises opportunities through systematic innovations.
1975 : Albert Shapero	:	entrepreneur takes initiative, organizes some socio-economic mechanisms, and accepts risk of failure.

1980 : Karl Vesper	:	entrepreneur seen differently by economists, psychologists, business persons, and politicians.
1983 : Giffor Pinchot	:	Intrapreneur is an entrepreneur within an already established organization.
1985 : Robert Hisrich	:	entrepreneur is the process of creating some-thing different with value by devoting the necessary time and effort, assuming the accompanying financial, psychological, and social risks and receiving the results-rewards of monetary personal satisfaction.
1990 : Vasant Desai	:	The entrepreneur brings in overall change through innovation for the maximum social good. Human values remain sacred and inspire him to serve society. He has firm belief in social betterment and he carries out this responsibility with conviction. In the process, he accelerates personal, economic as well as human development. The entrepreneur is a visionary and an integrated man with outstanding leadership qualities. With a desire to excel, the entrepreneur gives top priority to Research and Development. He always works for the well-being of the society. More importantly, entrepreneurial activities encompasses all fields/sectors and fosters a spirit of enterprise for the welfare of mankind.

The important phase of entrepreneurial development was after 1947. Entrepreneurship began to grow faster. The Government of India through industrial policy statements for rapid and balanced industrialization of the country. It recognized the responsibility of the State to promote, assist and develop industries in the national interest. It also recognized the vital role of the private sector in accelerating industrial devel̀opment. The Government decided to pursue the following objectives:

(i) Balance on Economic Powers. To maintain a proper distribution of economic power between private and public sectors;

(ii) Decentralization of Industries. To encourage the tempo of industrialization by spreading entrepreneurship from the existing centres to other cities, towns and villages; and

(iii) Dispersion of Entrepreneurial Spirit to All Section of Society. To disseminate the entrepreneurial acumen concentrated in a few dominant communities to a large number of industrially potential people of varied social strata.

Thus to achieve the above objectives the Government decided to encourage the development of small scale industries. It began to provide various incentives and concessions to small scale industries in the form of capital, technical know-how, markets and land to establish industries particularly in the backward regions of the country.

Industrial entrepreneurship prior to 1850 was negligible lying dormant in artisans. The artisan entrepreneurship could not develop due to inadequate infrastructure and negative attitude of the colonial rulers. From 1850 onwards, the East India Company, the managing agency houses, the Swadeshi Movement and the policy of encouraging small scale industries after independence provided seedbed for the emergence of manufacturing entrepreneurs. The family entrepreneurship units like Tata, Birla, Mafatlal, Dalmia, Singhania, Kirloskar and others came into existence.

Environmental Factors Influencing Entrepreneurship

Entrepreneurship does not emerge and grow spontaneously. It is dependent upon several economic, social, political and psychological factors. The environmental factors may have both positive and negative influences on the growth of entrepreneurship. Positive influences imply facilitating and conducive conditions whereas negative influences refer to factors inhibiting the emergence of entrepreneurship. Various environmental factors influencing the emergence of entrepreneurship are as: (1) Economic factors, (2) Social factors, (3) Psychological factors and (4) Government:

1. *Economic Conditions.* Economic environment exercises perhaps the most direct and immediate influence on entrepreneurship. Capital, labour, raw materials and markets are the main economic factors.

Capital. Capital is one of the most important prerequisites to establish an enterprise. Availability of capital facilitates the entrepreneur to bring together the labour of one, machine of another and raw material of yet another to combine them to produce goods. Capital is, therefore, regarded as a lubricant to the process of production. The timely and adequate supply of capital increases entrepreneurship. Example of France and Russia justify how lack of capital for industrial pursuits speedup the entrepreneurship.

The Good Quality of Labour Force. The good quality of working force is another factor which need attention and influences the emergence of entrepreneurship. It is seen cheap labour is less mobile, the favourable advantage of cheap labour is that these can stay more hours on work and will remain on duty as and when needed even on holidays. It appears that the labour problem clearly does not prevent entrepreneurship from emerbing. For example, the problem of low-cost immobile labour can circumvented by plunging ahead with capital-intensive technologies, as Germany did. It can be dealt with utilizing labour-intensive methods like Japan, for example. By contrast, the disadvantages of high-cost labour can be modified by introduction of labour-saving innovations as was done in the USA. Thus, it appears that labour problems can be solved more easily than capital can be created.

Raw Materials. The necessity of raw materials hardly needs any emphasis for establishing any industrial activity and, therefore, its influence in the emergence of entrepreneurship. In the absence of raw materials, neither any enterprise can be established nor an entrepreneur can be emerged. Of course, in some cases, technological innovations can compensate for raw material inadequacies. The Japanese case, for example, witnesses that lack of raw material clearly does not prevent entrepreneurship from emerging but influenced the direction in which entrepreneurship took place. In fact, the supply of raw material is not influenced by themselves but becomes influential depending upon other opportunity conditions.

Market. The fact remains that the potential of the market constitutes the major determinant of probable rewards from entrepreneurial function. The size and composition of market both influence entrepreneurship in their own ways. Practically, monopoly in a particular product in the market becomes more influential for entrepreneurship than a competitive market. Generally improvement in transportation is more beneficial to heavy industry than to light industry because of their effects on the movement of raw materials. Instances of sudden rather than gradual improvement in market potential provide the clearest evidence of the influence of this factor. Some experts refer to Germany and Japan as prime examples where rapid improvement in market was followed by rapid entrepreneurial appearance.

2. *Social Factors.* No one can under-rate the social environment in a country exercises a significant impact on the

emergence of entrepreneurship. The main components of social environment are as follows:

(i) Legitimacy of Entrepreneurship. The proponents of non-economic factors give emphasis to the relevance of a system of norms and values within a socio-cultural setting for the emergence of entrepreneurship. While Schumpeter recognizes the importance of such legitimacy in terms of appropriate social climate for entrepreneurship; Cochran calls it cultural themes and sanctions. The social status of those playing entrepreneurial role has been considered one of the most important contents of entrepreneurial legitimacy. One should believe that entrepreneurship will be more likely to emerge in settings in which legitimacy is high. There are others too who took the opinion that entrepreneurship can emerge even when entrepreneurial legitimacy is low or even negative provided that the government actions can overcome the negative orientations.

(ii) Social Mobility. Social mobility involves the degree of mobility, both social and geographical, and the nature of mobility channels within a system. The opinion that social mobility is crucial for entrepreneurial emergence is not unanimous. Some hold the view that a high degree of mobility is conductive to entrepreneurship. Both need for "openness" of a system and need for "flexibility" in role relations imply the need for the possibility of mobility within a system of entrepreneurship development. In contrast, there is another group of scholars who express the view that a lack of mobility possibly promotes entrepreneurship. Some even speak of entrepreneurship as coming through the crevices in a rigid social system.

Another opinion is a combination of the first two. A system should neither be too rigid nor too flexible. If it is too flexible, then individual will gravitate towards other roles. If it is too rigid, entrepreneurship will be restricted along with other activities.

Security. Several scholars have advocated entrepreneurial security as an important facilitator of entrepreneurial behaviour. Yet, scholars are not consensus on the amount of security that is needed. While Cole suggests 'minimal' security, McClelland speaks of 'moderate' certainty, for example. However, Peterson and Berger maintain that entrepreneurship is more likely to emerge under turbulent conditions than under conditions of equilibrium. Redlich provides the middle position in this regard when he suggests that insecurity does not hinder entrepreneurship, but rather that different kinds of insecurity will result in different kinds of entrepreneurship.

One regard security to be a significant factor for entrepreneurship development. This is reasonable too because if individuals are fearful of losing their economic assets or being subjected to various negative sanctions, they will not be inclined to increase their insecurity by behaving entrepreneurially.

3. *Psychological Factors.* Many entrepreneurial theorists have propounded theories of entrepreneurship that concentrate specifically upon psychological factors. We consider these theories separately for that reason.

Need Achievement. To the best of our knowledge, the best known of primarily psychological theories is David McClelland's 'theory of need achievement'. According to McClelland, a constellation of personal characteristics.

Withdrawal of Status Respect. Hagen attributed the withdrawal of status respect of a group to the genesis of entrepreneurship. Giving a very brief sketch of history of Japan, he concludes that she developed sooner than any non-Western society except Russia due to two historical differences. First, Japan had been free from 'colonial disruption' and secondly, the repeated long continued withdrawal of expected status form important groups (Samurai) in her society drove them to retreatism which caused them to emerge alienated from traditional values with increased creativity. This fact led them to the technological progress. Stonequist has also emphasized that technological innovations are caused more by the culturally marginal persons than others. He refers to Jews, Greeks and such persons in the middle ages, for example.

Hagen believes that the initial condition leading to eventual entrepreneurial behaviour is the loss of status by a group. He postulates that four types of events can produce status withdrawal:

(a) the group may be displaced by force;

(b) it may have its valued symbols denigrated;

(c) it may drift into a situation of status inconsistency;

(d) it may not be accepted into expected status on migration in a new society.

Hagen postulates that withdrawal of status respect would give rise to four possible reactions and create four different personality types:

(a) *Retreatist.* He who continues to work in a society but remains indifferent to his work and position;

(b) *Ritualist.* He who adopts a kind of defensive behaviour and acts in the way accepted and approved in his society but no hopes of improving his position;

(c) *Reformist.* He is a person who foments a rebellion and attempts to establish a new society; and

(d) *Innovator.* He is a creative individual and is likely to be an entrepreneur.

Hagen maintains that once status withdrawal has occurred, the sequence of change in personality formation is set in motion. He infers that status withdrawal takes a long period of time as much as five or more generations to result in the emergence of entrepreneurship.

4. *Governmental Influence.* The government by its actions or its failure to act does influence both the economic and non-economic conditions for entrepreneurship. Any interested government in economic development can help, through its clearly expressed industrial policy; promote entrepreneurship in one way or other, creating basic facilities, utilities and services and by providing incentives and concessions, the government can provide the prospective entrepreneurs a facilitative socio-economic setting. Such conducive setting minimises the risks which the entrepreneurs are to encounter. Thus, the supportive actions of the government appear as the most conducive to the entrepreneurial growth.

After discussing various factors which may be useful or otherwise for the emergence to entrepreneurs, an effort is made to give a comparative study of factors which favours the emergence to entrepreneurs and side by side the factors which may act as barriers to the growth of entrepreneurs are as:

Factors Influencing Entrepreneurship

Facilitating factors to the emergence of entrepreneurs:	*Barriers to the emergence of entrepreneurs*
(1)	*(2)*
1. Technical knowledge supply	1. Lack of technical skills
2. Entrepreneurial training facilities	2. Lack of proper market
3. Market contacts through Govt.	3. Lack of capital
4. Family business	4. Lack of business knowledge
5. Availability of capital from sources	5. Social stigma

Contd.

(1)	(2)
6. Successful role models	6. Time pressures and discussions
7. Cheap manpower	7. Legal and bureaucratical constraints on the Government part
8. Capable advisors and supporters	8. Political instability
9. Governmental and institutional.	9. Non cooperative attitude of banks and other support financial institutions.

Institutional Development Programmes for Entrepreneurship

Entrepreneurs are not necessarily born they can be developed through education, training and experience. Development of entrepreneurs means inculcating entrepreneurial skills required for setting up and operating business units. Entrepreneurial development is an organized and ongoing process. Its basic purpose is to motivate persons for entrepreneurial career and to make them capable of perceiving and exploiting business opportunities. Entrepreneurship development is not merely a training programme. It is the process of

1. Enhancing the motivation, knowledge and skills of potential entrepreneurs;
2. Arousing and reforming the entrepreneurial behaviour in their day-to-day activities; and
3. Assisting them in developing their own ventures.

An entrepreneurial development programme consists of the following phases:

(i) Pre-training Phase. This phase involves the following activities:

(a) Selection of persons with the required potential in terms of knowledge, attitudes, motivation and desire to go up.

(b) Creation of infrastructure for training.

(c) Preparing contents of the training programme.

(d) Designing techniques for training.

(e) Selection and training of the trainers.

(f) Survey of environment where these are to be trained.

(ii) *Development Phase.* During this phase the training programme is launched in order to carry out the necessary change in the skills, attitudes and behaviour of the participants.

(iii) *Post-training Phase.* This phase involves assessing the effectiveness of the training. Monitoring and follow up will reveal shortcomings in the training programme. Steps can then be taken to make the programme more effective. In this phase infrastructural support, counselling and assistance in establishing enterprises can be reviewed.

Institutions for Entrepreneurship Development

In our country there are several organizations engaged in entrepreneurship development programmes. Some of these are given below:

1. *The National Institute for Entrepreneurship and Small Business Development (NIESBUD), New Delhi.* It is an apex body for coordinating and overseeing the activities of different agencies engaged in entrepreneurial development. Its main functions are as follows:

(a) evolving effective training strategies and methodology;

(b) standardizing model syllabus for training various target groups;

(*c*) formulating scientific selection procedures;

(*d*) developing training aids, manuals and other tools;

(*e*) facilitating and supporting agencies engaged in entrepreneurship development;

(*f*) conducting such programmes which are not undertaken by other agencies;

(*g*) maximizing their benefits and accelerating the process of entrepreneurship development;

(*h*) organizing all those activities that help develop entrepreneurial culture in society.

NIESBUD is also the secretariat for the National Entrepreneurship Development Board (NEDB) the apex body which determines policy for entrepreneurship development in India.

2. *Entrepreneurship Development Institute of India (EDII), Ahmedabad.* It is an all India institution set by public financial institutions and the Gujarat Government. Its entrepreneurship development programme is quite comprehensive and successful consisting of the following steps:

(*a*) selecting potential entrepreneurs

(*b*) achievement motivation training

(*c*) product selection and project report preparation

(*d*) business management training

(*e*) practical training and work experience

(*f*) post training support and follow-up

EDII also conducts research and publications in the area of entrepreneurship development.

3. *National Alliance of Young Entrepreneurs (NAYE).* NAYE has sponsored several schemes of entrepreneurial development in collaboration with public sector banks. Some of these schemes are as follows:

(i) *Bank of India-NAYE.* This scheme known as BINEDS was sponsored in August 1972: It is operative in the States of Punjab, Rajasthan, and Himachal Pradesh, J & K, Chandigarh and Delhi.

(ii) *Dena Bank-NAYE.* This scheme is designed to promote ancillary units and small scale firms in Madras.

(iii) *Punjab National Bank.* This entrepreneurial assistance scheme was started in March 1977 in the States of West Bengal and Bihar.

(iv) *Central Bank of India-NAYE.* This entrepreneurial development programme is implemented in Maharashtra.

(v) *Union Bank of India-NAYE.* This scheme was introduced in June 1975 in Tamilnadu.

The main objective of these schemes are to help young entrepreneurs in identifying investment and self-employment opportunities, securing proper arrangements for their training induding development of their manufacturing capacities, providing necessary financial assistance on the basis of properly prepared reports, securing package of consultancy services on appropriate terms and arranging for all possible assistance, facilities, incentives being extended to young entrepreneurs by Government and other institutions.

4. *Indian Investment Centre (IIC).* It is an autonomous non-profit organization financed and supported by the Government of India. It seeks to promote mutually rewarding joint ventures between Indian and foreign entrepreneurs. It acts as a clear house of information to foreign investors, who

want to make investment in India. It functions as a link between Indian and foreign industrialists and assists them in entering into collaborations.

The IIC has setup an Entrepreneurial Guidance Bureau (EGB) to guide entrepreneurs in identifying investment opportunities, assisting them in selecting location, preparing project profiles, arranging financial assistance, etc. It maintains direct contacts with technically qualified persons and small entrepreneurs to promote entrepreneurial development.

5. *Technical Consultancy Organization (TCOs).* All India financial institutions and State Governments have setup a network of technical consultancy organizations in the country. These organizations provide a comprehensive package of services to potential entrepreneurs. Their main functions are as follows:

(i) Conducting surveys on industrial potential

(ii) Preparing project profiles and feasibility studies

(iii) Undertaking techno-economic appraisal of projects

(iv) Evaluating projects referred by financial institutions

(v) Carrying out marketing research

(vi) Providing technical and managerial assistance to entrepreneurs

(vii) Assisting entrepreneurs in modernization, technology upgradation and rehabilitation programmes.

(viii) Organizing information cell and data bank concerning industrial and economic activities and providing information for the development of industries to entrepreneurs.

(ix) Advising on setting up and organizing laboratories, design centres and machine shops and workshops, standardization units, etc.

In the field of entrepreneurial training TCOs identify potenial entrepreneurs, train them and render post-training counselling and guidance in selecting projects and establishing industrial units.

6. *Commercial Banks.* Most of the public sector banks are conducting entrepreneurship development programmes with a view to identify potential entrepreneurs especially in backward area, and training and monitoring them in starting new ventures. Some banks have created entrepreneurship service cells or guidance bureaus, for this purpose. Commercial banks prepare several functions to assist and encourage small entrepreneurs. Some of these are:

(a) assistance in judging the technical and commercial viability of project proposals.

(b) assistance in preparing and evaluating project reports

(c) practical training in the selected industry

(d) assistance in procuring machinery and equipment

(e) assistance in obtaining Government clearances

(f) assistance in raising the required funds

(g) assistance and guidance in implementing the project, etc.

Entrepreneurial Performance in India

According to Dr. R.A. Sharma entrepreneurial performance is a function of the following factors:

(a) Motivational Force (MF). It implies the motives which prompt a person to undertake entrepreneurship *e.g.* wealth, status, self-employment, etc.

(b) Knowledge and Ability of the Entrepreneur (KA). It refers to the education, training and experience of the entrepreneur.

(c) Socio-cultural Background of the Entrepreneur (SB). This implies the environment in which the entrepreneur was born and brought up. It conditions the values and attitudes of the entrepreneur.

(d) Financial Strength (FS). It means the funds which an entrepreneur can mobilize from internal and external sources.

(e) Environmental Variables (EV). These consist of Government policies market conditions, availability of technology and labour situation. Symbolically

$$EP = f\ (SB, MF, KA, FS \text{ and } EV)$$

Where EP represents entrepreneurial performance.

Several studies have been conducted to judge the performance of Indian entrepreneurs. The main criteria used to judge performance of entrepreneurs are as follows:

1. *Gestation Period.* It is defined as the time gap between the date of incorporation and the date of commencement of commercial production. Financial institutions consider the performance of an enterprise as satisfactory if it starts commercial production within two or three years of its establishment. Generally executives technicians and professionals had lesser gestation period than traders. Reasons cited for delay in project implementation were Government approvals, assistance from financial institutions, non-availability of suitable manpower, delayed supply of plant and machinery, delay in constitution of factory buildings non-cooperation from collaborators, etc.

2. *Financial Results.* Total assets or gross block representing the physical expansion of an enterprise was used. In order to judge financial health of units, return on capital employed, net profit over sales, net profit over net worth and other ratios were used.

3. *Expansion and Diversification.* Expansion was defined as increase in the installed capacity. Diversification was defined as taking up production of new products. All the units achieving full capacity utilization tried for expansion and some of them opted for diversification.

4. *Capacity Utilization.* It depends upon the availability of required inputs like raw materials, power, labour, etc. and market for the finished product. About 50 per cent of the entrepreneurs utilized 80 per cent capacity. Most of the entrepreneurs could break even at 60% of the installed capacity.

5. *Value Added by Manufacture.* It is a measure of a firm's contribution to the national income. It implies gross value of output minus the value of raw materials and other intermediate inputs used in the production process. It can be used as an indicator of entrepreneurial abilities such as preparedness to assume higher degree of risk and ability to plan and operate relatively large firms.

6. *Growth of Offspring Enterprises.* The number of ancillaries that have originated from a unit was taken as a manifestation of growth. But it is not necessary that all entrepreneurs set up offspring enterprises for growth.

7. *Others.* Several other factors can be used to judge entrepreneurial performance. Sales turnover, size of employment generated, volume of exports, research and development activity, import substitution, rural development are some of these factors.

8

TYPES OF ENTREPRENEUR

A number of factors are responsible for driving a person to entrepreneurship and his becoming an entrepreneur. However, in case of every individual some factors play a greater role than others. Based upon their motivating factors entrepreneurs can easily be classified into three types as Spontaneous, Motivated and Induced entrepreneurs.

Spontaneous Entrepreneurs. These entrepreneurs are motivated by their desire for self-fulfilment and to achieve or prove their excellence in job performance. They are the natural entrepreneurs in any society and generally do not need any external motivation. Their strength lies in their creative abilities, which leads them to set up innovative business ventures. Such entrepreneurs can normally be identified while they are young and are fired by an ambition to be their own boss.

Motivated Entrepreneurs. These entrepreneurs are motivated by their desire to make use of their technical and professional expertise and skills. They have confidence in their abilities, posses initiative and boldness, are highly ambitious and are normally not satisfied by the slow progress in their jobs. A small dose of any of the compelling reasons discussed above and a little support motivates them to start their enterprise. They come into being because of the possibility of providing some new product or service to the consumers. If the customers accept the product or service, the financial rewards further motivate the entrepreneurs. However, they are equally likely to set up innovative or imitative business ventures.

Induced Entrepreneurs. Induced entrepreneurs are those who are induced to take up entrepreneurship due to policy measures of the government promoting entrepreneurship. Generally, governments provide assistance, incentives, concessions and other facilities like infrastructure support to people setting up new ventures. Sometimes prospective entrepreneurs are induced or even forced by their special circumstances, such as loss of job or inability to find a job suitable for their talent, to adapt to entrepreneurship. Till a few years back, import restrictions and reservation of certain products for Small Scale Sector induced a large number of entrepreneurs to set up their small scale units. Presently venture funds are inducing the successful IT professionals to become entrepreneurs.

Difference between Innovation and Research

How innovation differs from the two other notions with which it is sometimes confused research mid invention.

Meaning of Research. The aim of research is to produce knowledge, whereas innovation to produce objects which work and can be sold. Since it is inspired by different objectives.

Meaning of Innovation. Innovation may be based on the application of knowledge produced by research but it may also be purely empirical: indeed practice often precedes theory and innovation may open the way to research (the steam engine for thermodynamics, or the computer for programming). Moreover, many innovations are not based on research but on ingenious combinations of existing materials and components.

Steps to Improved Innovation. Innovation means differently to different people. For some, it means new product ideas or new manufacturing processes that lower delivered costs. The manager may define it broadly as a strategic and profitable management of change. Still others think in terms of developmental stages: idea, implementation and diffusion throughout the market place. Many entrepreneurs appreciate the need for innovative thinking and implementation in every area, from human resources management to transportation. All these require special planning, implementation, and control. More importantly, the entrepreneurs today recognize that careful management of innovation can go a long way towards assuring real growth, competitiveness and profitability.

Arthur Young and the Institute for Innovation have created a group of powerful analytical tools that assist the entrepreneurs to innovate and change.

Steps	Innovation—Management
One	Understanding
Two	Recogition
Three	Aanalysis
Four	Reviewing
Five	Measuring
Six	Evaluation
Seven	Determination
Eight	Improving
Nine	Developing
Ten	Implementation & Monitoring

If small business in the developed countries has received special attention it is because it has been the fountainhead of innovation and creativity. Studies have brought out that a large number of innovations have come from small, rather than large business. As these innovative firms entered the market they made profits and created jobs. In the US, Presidents Jimmy Carter and Gerald Ford emphasized that small business created 60 per cent of the new jobs in the United States. And this employment generation was due to its better financial performance. Similarly, the Bolton Committee, 1971, and the Wilson Committee, 1979. also concluded that the small business in the UK had higher profitability than large business.

The studies on entrepreneurship also point out that, "most of the risk in entrepreneurial management lies not in misperception of opportunity, but in trying to pursue opportunity, without adequate resources. One of the fundamental errors of large corporations, on the other hand, is over commitment of resources".

Economists' View. In economic analysis, entreprenturial functions are supposed to be directed towards the materialistic objective of maximization though its foundations may be of a high order such as spiritual, patriotic, social, psychological or ethnic. Entrepreneurial activity is a form-giving activity giving form to the wishes of the society, to ideals, to the efforts of factors and to the raw material to be processed through.

J.S. Mill lists superintendence, control and direction as entrepreneurial functions. Superintendence: to assemble the means, turn out-of maximum at minimum cost and to supervise the work. Control: the flow of goods, use of finance, utilization of machinery and the activities of the subordinates. Direction : he is a goal-oriented person; he has to keep the organization constantly on the path of his objective. He is an activity of producing in present what the future will demand. Mill emphasizes managerial and administrative functions of an entrepreneur according to Marshall. Organization building capacity is the most critical skill expected of an entrepreneur.

He assigns to the entrepreneur the functions of risk-bearing, innovation and management. To Cantillon, an entrepreneur is an uncertainty-bearer buying at a fixed price and selling at an uncertain one.

Kirzner viewed the entrepreneur as a disequilibrating force. It is the alertness to unnoticed opportunities which creates a tendency of the ever circular flow of equilibrium. Harvey Leibenstein states, "Entrepreneur is an individual or group of individuals with four major characteristics. He connects different markets; he is capable of making market deficiencies (gap-filling); he is input complete and he creates or expands time-binding, input-transforming entities. (firms)."

B.F. Hoselitz reports, "The primary function of entrepreneurship is the investment of time, capital and energy in economically significant pursuits: the emphasis is on decision-making in its various aspects." Harbinson enumerates four functions: the undertaking or managing of risks and handling of economic uncertainty; planning and innovation; coordination, administration and control, routine supervision. Ability to build organization is, perhaps, Harbinson adds, the most precious of an entrepreneurial skills. Redlich's three-fold division of function is: (1) capitalist-employing the factors and buying raw material, setting up the organization. (2) managerial-innovation, supervision and coordination of productive activities; and (3) entrepreneurial decision-making. Benjamin Higgins lists seeing opportunities for introduction of new techniques, new products and exploitation of new resources and organizing factors of production into an enterprise to take advantage of these opportunities as essential for economic development.

Economic functions described above isolate the entrepreneur from the economic environs, social milieu and political ethos in which he functions. Maximization is taken as the pole star in his voyage. It seems to be conveniently assumed that he is abundantly provided with all the resources and the market readily absorbs what he put into it. Reality is, however, full of bottlenecks and hurdles which are ignored in the above-mentioned works. Small industry is a natural habitat of the entrepreneur where his role is like that of a stoker who keeps the fire burning. Economic functioning takes no notice of this.

Sociologists' View. Sociologists consider the entrepreneur as a role performer corresponding to the role expected by the society. Wishes of the society are exhibited through customs and taboos, rewards and restraints, ethnic values and child-rearing practices, nationalistic attitude and patriotic inculcations and protestant ethics. He is conditioned by the social milieu to which he belongs. According to Peter Marris, to assemble or reassemble from what is available, very concrete kind of imagination, to see what others have missed, sensitivity to business and social environment, zest in industrial development and entrepreneurial courage are the factors that make an entrepreneur. According to Flavia Derossi: *(i)* coordination at every stage, *(ii)* inception, maintenance and expansion is the function of an entrepreneur. She feels two qualities: (1) Optimistic outlook that there is a possibility of change, the environrrent can be mastered and he himself can introduce the required change. He finds difficulties challenging and stimulating; he thrives on them. (2) In a share as dynamic industry, new problems are seized upon as opportunities for testing one's own capabilities.

Psychologists' View. Psychologists, Frank Young describes an entrepreneur as a change-agent, entrepreneurs are men who exhibit qualities of leadership in solving persistent professional problems; but those persons likewise demonstrate eagerness to seize unusual opportunities. Udai Pareek describes entrepreneurship as creative and innovative response to environment. The entrepreneur is goal-oriented rather than means-oriented. He must not only have a high capacity of risk-taking but must also have a high capacity of risk-sustaining which is a function of a high degree of self-confidence.

Thus, the foregoing description of the functions of an entrepreneur presents the profile of a functionary. Economists present him as a perceiver of otherwise unnoticed opportunity, organization builder, adapter of new profitable activity and beneficiary thereof. Sociologists present him as a personality moulded by various practice of social enforcement and values imbibed in him. Psychologically, entrepreneurship is a vigorous application of the person's energies towards the long-cherished goals of any organization.

Classification of Entrepreneurs

The entrepreneurs in business broadly classified according to the types of business, use of professional skill, motivation, growth and stages of development. The various types of entrepreneurs are as follows:

According to the Type of Business

Entrepreneurs are found in various types of business occupations of varying size are as:

1. *Business Entrepreneurs.* Business entrepreneurs are individuals who conceive an idea for a new product or service and then create a business to materialize their idea into reality. They tap both production and marketing resources in their search to deveiop a new business opportunity. They may set up a big establishment or a small business unit. They are called small business entrepreneurs when found in small business units such as printing press, textile processing house, advertising agency, readymade garments, or confectionery. In a majority of cases, entrepreneurs are found in small trading and manufacturing business and entrepreneurship flourishes when the size of the business is small.

2. *Trading Entrepreneur.* Entrepreneur who undertakes trading activities and is not concerned with the manufacturing work. He identifies potential markets, simulates demand for his product line and creates a desire and interest among buyers to go in for his product. He is engaged in both domestic and overseas trade. Britain, due to geographical limitations, has developed trade through trading entrepreneurs. These entrepreneurs demonstrated their ability in pushing many ideas ahead which promoted their business.

3. *Corporate Entrepreneur.* Corporate entrepreneur is a person who demonstrates his innovative skill in organizing and managing a corporate undertaking. A corporate undertaking is a form of business organization which is registered under some statue or Act which gives it a separate legal entity. A trust registered under the Trust Act, or a company registered under the Companies Act are examples of corporate undertakings. A corporate entrepreneur is thus an individual who plans, develops and manages a corporate body.

4. *Industrial Entrepreneur.* He is essentially a manufacturer who identifies the potential needs of customers and tailors product or service to meet the marketing needs. He is product-oriented man who starts in an industrial unit because of the possibility of making some new product. The entrepreneur has the ability to convert economic resources and technology into a considerably profitable venture. He is found in any industrial unit such as the electronic industry, textile units, machine tools or video cassette type plant and the like.

5. *Agricultural Entrepreneur.* Agricultural entrepreneurs are those entrepreneurs who undertake such agricultural activities as raising and marketing of crops, fertilizers and other input or agriculture. They are motivated to raise the productivity of agriculture through mechanization, irrigation and application of technologies for dry land agriculture. They

cover a broad spectrum of the agricultural sector and include agriculture and allied occupations.

According to the Use of Technology

The use of new technology in various sectors of the national economy is essential for the future growth of business. Thus, these entrepreneurs on the basis of the use of technology as follows:

1. *Technical Entrepreneur.* A technical entrepreneur is essentially an entrepreneur of "craftsman type." He develops new and improved quality of goods because of his craftsmanship. He concentrates more on production than marketing. He does not care much to generate sales by applying various sales promotional techniques. He demonstrates his innovative capabilities in matters of production of goods and rendering services. The greatest strength which the technical entrepreneur has is his skill in production techniques.

2. *Professional Entrepreneur.* Professional entrepreneur is a person who is interested in establishing a business but does not have interest in managing or operating it once it is established. A professional entrepreneur sells out the nmning business and starts another venture with the sales proceeds. Such an entrepreneur is dynamic and he conceives new ideas to develop alternative projects. In India, these were managing agents.

3. *Non-technical Entrepreneur.* Non-technical entrepreneurs are those who are not concerned with the technical aspects of the product in which they deal. They are concerned only with developing alternative marketing and distribution strategies to promote their business.

According to Motivation

Motivation is the force that influences the efforts of the entrepreneur to achieve his objectives. An entrepreneur is motivated to achieve or prove his excellence in job performance. He is also motivated to influence others by demonstrating his command on work.

1. *Pure Entrepreneur.* A pure entrepreneur is an individual who is motivated by psychological and economic rewards. He undertakes an entrepreneurial activity for his personal satisfaction in work, ego or status.

2. *Induced Entrepreneur.* Induced entrepreneur is one who is induced to take up an entrepreneurial task due to the policy measures of the government that provides assistancc, incentives, concessions and necessary overhead facilities to start a venture. Most of the entrepreneurs are induced entrepreneurs who enter business due to financial, technical and several other facilities provided to them by the state agencies to promote entrepreneurship. A person with a sound project is provided package assistance to his project. Today, import restrictions, and allocation of production quotas to small units have induced many people to start a small-scale industry.

3. *Spontaneous Entrepreneur.* These entrepreneurs start their business out of their natural talents. They are persons with initiative, boldness and confidence in their ability which motivate them to undertake entrepreneurial activity. Such entrepreneurs have a strong conviction and confidence in their ability.

4. *Motivated Entrepreneur.* New entrepreneurs are motivated by the desire for self-fulfilment. They come into being because of the possibility of making and marketing some new product for the use of consumers. If the product is developed to a saleable stage, the entrepreneur is further motivated by reward in terms of profit.

According to Growth

The development of a new venture has a greater chance of success. The entrepreneur enters a new and open field of business. The customer approval to the new product gives them psychological satisfaction and enormous profit. The industrial units are identified as high growth, medium growth and low growth industries and as such we have "Growth Entrepreneur" and Super Growth Entrepreneur."

1. *Growth Entrepreneur.* Growth entrepreneurs are those who necessarily take up a high growth industry. These entrepreneurs choose an industry which has substantial growth prospects.

2. *Super-Growth Entrepreneur.* Super-growth entrepreneurs are those who have shown enormous growth of performance in their venture. The growth performance is identified by the liquidity of funds, profitability and gearing.

According to Stages of Development

Entrepreneurs may also be classified as the first generation entrepreneur, modern entrepreneur and classical entrepreneur, depending upon the stage of development.

1. *First-Generation Entrepreneur.* A first-generation entrepreneur is one who starts an industrial unit by means of an innovative skill. He is essentially an innovator, combining different technologies to produce a marketable product or service.

2. *Classical Entrepreneur.* A classical entrepreneur is one who is concerned with the customers and marketing needs through the development of a self-supporting venture. He is a stereotype entrepreneur whose aim is to maximize his economic returns at a level consistent with the survival of the firm with or without an element of growth.

3. *Modern Entrepreneur.* A modern entrepreneur is one who undertakes those venture which go well along with the changing demand in the market. They undertake those ventures which suit the current marketing needs.

4. *Imitative Entrepreneurs.* Imitative entrepreneurship is characterised by readiness to adopt successful innovations by innovating entrepreneurs. They first imitate techniques and technology innovated by others.

5. *Innovating Entrepreneurs.* Innovating entrepreneurship is characterised by aggressive assemblage of information and analysis of results, deriving from a novel combination off actors. Men/women in this group are generally aggressive in experimentation who exhibit cleverness in putting attractive possibilities into practice. One need not invent but convert even old established products or services, by changing their utility, their value, their economic characteristics, into something new, attractive and utilitarian. Tern lies the key to their phenomenal success. Such an entrepreneur is one who sees the opportunity for introducing a new technique of production process or a new commodity or a new market or a new service or even reorganiation of an existing enterprise.

Indian Scene. In step with India's liberalization process, entrepreneurship has received a boost. In the last two decades, even the composition of entrepreneurial class has seen a sea change as an increasing number of a whole new class of entrepreneurs has been born. The new entrepreneur is educated; sometimes abroad, is keyed into the frontiers of technology, aware of the latest in the production techniques, generally conscious of current management systems and is relatively well versed in marketing and quality control. More importantly, this class of entrepreneurs are well spread all over the country and harvesting the fruits of liberalized economy.

❋❋❋

9

ENTREPRENEURIAL TRAINING

Training is an integral input of managerial development which train the hand and mind. The shortage of trained personnel is one of the serious problems in a developing economy. No one can deny this fact that training is needed for entrepreneurs and workers employed in small enterprises.

Meaning of Training. Training is the systematic instruction of staff at all levels in new attitudes or new skills. Mere learning job is not training, the term refers to scheme of instructions which is more or less formal and ongoing, which is planned, systematic, consistent, pervasive and monitored to measure its effectiveness.

Definition of Training. Following are the main definitions:

1. *Jucius.* The term training is used to indicate only a process, by which the aptitudes, skill, and capabilities of the employees to perform specific jobs are increased.

2. *Dale S. Breach.* Training is the organized procedure by which employees learn knowledge and skill for a definite purpose.

Training is needed to curb wastes and increase the efficiency of employees. Efficient staff, is not born but are created by training. New staff may need additionally a programme of training to enable them to obtain their professional qualification. Certain individuals may need training for a specific purpose, the development of a new service, taking on a new role in the organization, preparing for retirement. Training is that process through which an effort is made to increase abilities of the employees in some new jobs by addition in their knowledge and skill. The role of training is to develop the critical awareness of staff.

Importance of Training

The importance of training employees result in the following advantages:

1. *Availability of Trained Staff.* Training makes sure the availability of skilled workers at all levels of management.

2. *Improvement in Quality and Quantity of Work.* Training increases the potential abilities of employees and thus increases their work performance both in terms of quality and quantity. They work more efficiently and precisely so as to maintain quality of products.

3. *Reduction in Accidents.* Training minimizes the number of accidents as unskilled and semi-skilled are more prone to industrial accidents.

4. *Economies in Operation.* Training minimizes excessive scrap, defectives and wastage in the production process. A trained employee is always watchful while using material and machine.

5. *Lesser Labour Turnover.* Trained employees are satisfied withtheir quality and quantity of work done, consequently get more and more promotional avenues, reduces labour turnover.

6. *Lesser Supervision.* The trained employees become skilled or expert in their jobs, thus, they do not need more attention of their supervisors. Thus the supervisor can be used for some other useful purpose.

7. *Improvement in Adaptation.* Continuous training results in mental development of the employees and they become habitual of adapting to the latest technological changes. They develop an urge to learn the possible new changes.

8. *Check on Overtime Payment.* When the speed of the production increases, overtime work can be avoided and thus, the payment of overtime does not arise.

9. *Job Satisfaction.* An employee can get job satisfaction when he is proficient in his work, which can be achieved through training. Training not only gives job satisfaction but creates self-confidence in employees.

10. *Good Relation between Capital (Management) and Employees.* Major cause of industrial unrest is low wage rate to workers. Low wage is paid due to their poor efficiency. By giving them training efficiency is pumped and more perks are given thereby possibility of good relation between capital and labour is increased.

Objectives of Training

The training programme is designed to subserve the following objectives:

(i) To impart basic knowledge about the industry, production and production methods;

(ii) To build the necessary skills of new entrepreneurs and workers;

(iii) To assist the entrepreneur/worker to function more effectively in his present position by exposing him to the latest concept, techniques and information;

(iv) To expose the entrepreneur to the latest developments which directly or indirectly affect him;

(v) To build up second line of workers and prepare them to shoulder additional responsibility and/or

switch on the production of a new product, if there is any diversification;

(vi) To broaden the vision of entrepreneurs by providing them suitable opportunities for an interchange of experiences within and outside an industry;

(vii) To impart customer education;

(viii) To impart knowledge of the marketing of goods.

Principles of Training

The following are the main principles of training:

1. *Principle of Need.* Training should be given in a proper atmosphere and that too systematically oy qualified and trained instructor keeping in mind the need of the trainees.

2. *Principle of Reward.* The aim of training is to increase efficiency and work culture, with the result, profit will increase. Effort should be made to declare reasonable promotion, increase in salary and higher position before the commencement of the training. It will make training more successful.

3. *Principle of Individual Differences.* Training is given in groups. The group of trainees should be of similar capabilities as each individual has different level of understanding.

4. *Principle of Practicality.* Training should not stress on theory but it should be supplemented by practical training and efforts should be made to make it interesting.

5. *Principle of Repetition.* Once training is given it should be repeated after some time so that employees are refreshed. It will make them up-to-date.

6. *Principle of Planning.* Before training it should be well planned so that the level of training should be decided, it should be comprehensive and the participant should be made

familiar with the latest trend in production technology. It should be in a systematic way rather than in an unplanned manner.

7. *Principle of Economy.* An effort should be made to minimise the cost of training.

8. *Principle of Open Competition.* This principle refers to the new appointment in the organization through promotion, or from external sources. Thus to be in the open race employee should take extensive training otherwise outsiders will be taken and their claim will not be justified.

9. *Principle of Continuity.* Change is the law of nature, there are always new changes and challenges in business environment every day. An effort should be made at continuous training programme to make latest changes known to employees.

Designing an Entrepreneurship Training Programme

Designing the training programme involves setting training objectives, developing the course content and choosing appropriate training methods. The programme design is prescribed by the training needs of the target clientele. The training objectives should be stated clearty, be trainee-centred, employ observable action words can be concerned with ends rather than means. When objectives are set, the course content can be developed. The elements of content are knowledge, habits, skills and control of emotion. The material to be included should be accorded priority according to its relative degree of importance to achieving training objectives. Certain sequences can be followed in arranging the content. Developing the course content involves several steps, starting from analyzing training needs and stating outcomes. In choosing the appropriate training methods, the factors to be considered are the subject area, the nature of learning, the trainee population, the trainers themselves and time and material factors. There are three processes involved in designing the training programme: setting training objectives, developing the course content or curriculum, and choosing appropriate training methods.

Training Objectives. Training objectives are statements that describe what the trainees will be able to do upon completion of the training or at any designated point during the training. In other words, they represent the goals which the entrepreneur aims to reach. Once he has clearly decided where he wants to go, then it will be reasonably easy to determine how to achieve the goal.

Setting Training Objectives. The training objectives make up the framework of the programme on which other training decisions, including the course content itself as well as the methods to be used, will be based. Setting training objectives stems primarily from the results of the training needs assessment.

Developing Course Content. After the training objectives have been clearly set, the course content can be developed. While the training objectives serve as the skeletal framework of the course, the content represents its flesh and blood. It embodies the subject-matter or learning points that will be put across to enable the trainees to attain the training objectives.

Again, in formulating the content, the planner must be guided by the results of the training need assessment and analysis, and of course, by the training objectives.

The data on training need analysis will help the planner to identify the specific knowledge habits, skills, etc. that the trainees should acquire. Training objectives on the other hand will indicate the specific behaviour expected of the trainees at the end of the training.

Financial and Technical Support Programmes for Entrepreneurship Development. The financial problems cited by the entrepreneurs include lack of collateral/guarantor for obtaining loans, unorganized finance sectors which offer loans at higher interest rates, poor credit collection, in adequate loans, short repayment period, red tape and voluminous paper requirements.

Development of the Practice-oriented Training Programme. The aforementioned principle concepts and approaches can be projected upon the actual interventions that have taken place in the project area. The activities were developed in such a manner that it became gradually evident that the various steps to be taken and already taken were interrelated logically and reflected the methodology. The steps taken can be identified as follows:

(a) Identification of problems and prospects of general nature (in selected sectors).

  (i) general assessment;

  (ii) data collection;

  (iii) identification of problems and prospects of both the entrepreneur and the enterprise.

(b) Identification of specific problems and prospects.

  (i) By enterprise in selected sectors by means of action survey techniques (a continuous process).

(c) Identification of (technical) resources available, a process undertaken simultaneously with *(b)*.

(d) Forming groups of participants/trainers.

(e) Execution and implementation of work plan (also is a continuous process).

(f) Follow-up and evaluation. (see also the structure given)

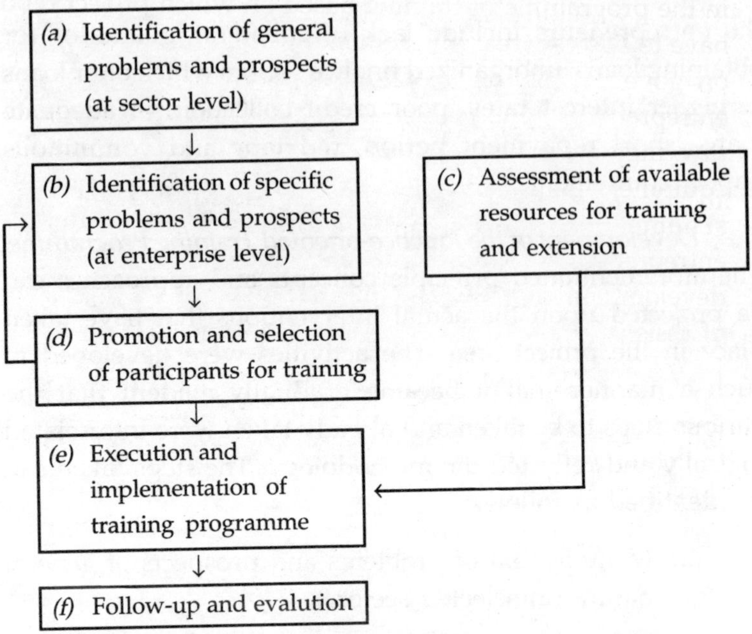

Building up an Action-Oriented Training Programme

Entrepreneurship Development Training. The progranune of training in entrepreneurship development is to develop motivation of potential entrepreneurs, help them in taking up suitable enterprises and activities, enable them to prepare economically viable and technically feasible project reports and enhance their enterprise-building skills. The motivational inputs include psychological games, tests, goal setting exercise and role play. The objective of these inputs is to enable the participants to understand their own entrepreneurial personality and behaviour and bring about through self study changes in self concept; values, and skills leading to positive entrepreneurial behaviour.

The training programme enables entrepreneurs to develop skills in identifying suitable items for manufacture or other self-employment ventures. The technique of conducting studies, market surveys and research should further be covered in the programme of training based on which project reports have to be prepared. For organizing an industry, information on government policies and programmes is helpful to the entrepreneurs. A number of institutional agencies offer finance, raw materials, ready-made sheds, power, machinery and equipment and water etc. Some states have also introduced schemes of incentives and concessions available to entrepreneurs. A programme for training for entrepreneurship development should also cover information on programmes of assistance and support system.

The training programme should not only develop proper entrepreneurial motivation and skill for project preparation but should also ensure that entrepreneurs are able to develop their enterprises well by application of scientific managerial techniques in various fields of management. The managerial contents of programme of training should be considered as vital for developing enterprise-building skills and various aspects of management such as: financial management, marketing management, production management, inventory control, labour laws and taxation laws should be covered in the programme. There is also the need for visits to the industrial units, consistent with the items identified by the entrepreneurs to gain more knowledge on production processes and machines required for the purpose. Facilities for in-plant training will further heighten the usefulness of the programme, particularly when the enterprises are very small or in areas where there is paucity of skilled personnel. Thus entrepreneurship is a movement for motivation and development of knowledge and skill.

Methods of Training

The following are the important methods by which training may be imparted.

1. *Individual Instruction.* Under this method, a single individual is selected for training. This mode of training is

undertaken where a complicated skill is to be taught to an individual.

2. *Group Instruction.* This mode of training is suitable for a group of individuals who have to perform similar type of work and where general instructions as applicable to all are to be given.

3. *Lecture Method.* Here the instructor orally communicates the practice to be followed by the learners. Under this method, whenever there are any doubts, they may be clarified on the spot.

4. *Demonstration Method.* Where the performance of work is to be shown physically by the instructor for better understanding, this method can be followed. This is more concerned with the practical than theoretical aspect.

5. *Conference.* Conferences are frequently organized where in experts in the field share their ideas and bring to the notice of learners the new ideas and techniques that can be used to increase production.

6. *Written Instructional Method.* This medium of training is followed where a future reference is to be made by the learners. This method is mostly followed where a standardised production system is followed.

7. *Meetings.* Meetings are a mode of training involving a group of people who discuss the various problems confronting them. They involve exchanging ideas and views and later on, coming to a firm conclusion based on the various proposals and alternatives.

Small-scale industries in India suffer from various handicaps compared to large-scale industries; one of the most important among these is the non-availability of technical and managerial personnel of the required calibre. Large industries can employ qualified staff who are specialised in different areas of pruduction and management. Further, they can afford to retain from time to time their own supervisory personnel and workers. Whereas the small industrialist cannot afford to employ workers and supervisors having a sound educational background and the requisite experience in production and in trade. Besides, they do not have the equipment and resources to train their own staff. To meet this lacuna, the training of small industrialists and their workers has been taken up as an important part of the Industrial Extension Service rendered by the Development Commissioner, Small-Scale Industries Organizations. The courses provided are designed to familiarise small industrialists and their workers with the latest tools and techniques in their respective fields. The object of the training of personnel for and from small scale industries is to equip them with improved management/ technical know-how and to apprise them of the kinds of assistance available from various government organizations. The training programme of such personnel is suitably geared to the need of individuals with different background and performing different functions.

Staff Training

- Basic Knowledge
- Skills
- Effective Work
- Vision
- Productivity

The training of instructors at various levels was *sine qua* non of the programme. Besides training officers of the DCSSIO, it became imperative that State Government officers, entrusted with the development of small-scale industries, should be given similar training, since the development of small industries is a State subject under the Constitution. Indeed, the training programmes of this organization commenced within orientation training for its own officers in change of the Pilot (industrial) Projects under the Community Development Programme. The Small-Scale Industries Organization has extended the benefit of its training resources and programmes to other developing countries which, being interested in the development programmes of small-scale industries, have been deputing their officers for participation in training programmes, study visits, etc., specially arranged by it for them.

In the post-independence period the nation laid stress and put its faith in science and technology. The country has made tremendous investments in scientific institutions and scientific and technical manpower. These investments need to be harvested. We have learnt that the managerial skills necessary to harvest business are different from the skills required to create business. Similarly, to create technology enterprises we may also require different kinds of managers in our science and technology institutions. Development of technical entrepreneurship and the management of science and technology cannot be dealt with in mutual exclusion.

Training in Technical Trades. Regular and ad hoc training courses in various technical trade are conducted by Small Industries Services Institutes, Branch SISI's Extension Centres and Production Centres for Artisans, both skilled and semi-skilled, sponsored by small-scale industries for upgrading their existing skills and broadening their areas of competence to meet the specific requirements of small-scale industries.

Entrepreneurial Development Programme. The Entrepreneurial Development Programmes are broadly classified into two categories, namely *(a)* Motivation campaigns for identification and selection of entrepreneurs, and *(b)* Entrepreneurial Development Training Programmes for the target groups with a new thrust for the development of industries in the backward and rural areas. The Small Industries Development Organization (SIDO) operates varied EDP activities and through its nation-wide network of SISIs specialised exclusive institutes and the State level Entrepreneurship Development Institutes to train more entrepreneurs.

❋❋❋

10

ENTREPRENEURIAL BEHAVIOURS AND MOTIVATION

A state of need is a motive, the action initiated or the drive behaviour is known as motivated and attainment of needs and reduction of drive by the achievement of goal is known, as the "process of motivation". Motivation in general is an important determinant for entrepreneurial growth and development in society. However, under the broad spectrum of motivation, certain social motives have been found to be significantly related to entrepreneurial behaviour such as the need for achievement, power, affiliation, dependency, extension, personal achievement, social achievement, influence, etc. Among all these motives, three catagories of social motives seem to be extensively ex-plored. These are the need for (1) achievement, (2) power and (3) affiliation.

These categories of social motives differ from each other in terms of satisfaction desired in undertaking activities as well as in terms of thoughts, feelings and actions of the individual.

Entrepreneurial motivation, therefore may be viewed in terms of a set of motives of varying strength such as a high need to achieve, moderate need for power and low affiliation motive. Apart from the motivational profile, other behavioural dimensions like tolerance to ambiguity, problem-solving, creativity etc., adds in building entrepreneurial motivation in a larger perspective. Among these motives, the achievement motive acquires a strategic and important position, and for this reason it is often equated with entrepreneurial motivation which is quite close but is not the same.

People create enterprises in order to grow and fulfil themselves *i.e.,* for Self-Fulfilment. Abraham Maslow has referred to this need as "Self-actualization", a need to maximize one's potential, whatever it may be. It is a desire to become what one is capable of becoming. A person normally does not become an entrepreneur for affiliation or recognition, but to achieve what he thinks he is capable of. This urge to self-actualization is common to all human.

The drive for self-actualization is frequently more apparent in children than in adults, probably because as adults we have learned to contain our desires. To some extent we have blocked off our innate drives and urges. Maslow went further and distinguished between "special talent creativeness" and "self-actualizing creativeness". While special talent creativeness might be focused on, say, musical or artistic activities, self-actualizing creativeness can just as easily be displayed in innovative and entrepreneurial pursuits.

Human begins are naturally creative and innovative. However, all successful innovators have to learn to overcome the emotional, perceptual and cultural barriers, which prevent them from testing and implementing their ideas.

The main function of managers is to achieve predetermined objectives of the organization by organizing the activities of individuals working in the organization. Human factor in production has an important role in the organization. The main question to take action is how to utilise the availability of human resources efficiently. The efficiency of a person depends upon.

(i) The level of ability to do a certain work, and

(ii) The willingness to do the work.

Thus, the factor number one can be acquired by education and training the second factor can be created by motivation.

It is important to understand the ability to do a work and willingness to work are two different qualities. A qualified person can be appointed on the basis of his ability to do certain work and further can be increased by training. The more important for the managers how the willingness to do the work can be affected. To harness their latent capability has to be ignited by the use of motivation.

Whenever a person does some work there is always a need behind it which motivates him in doing so. This impelling need is called motive. Under motivation, the will to do a work is aroused among the people by making them feel the motive behind their work. Motivation is derived from the word 'motive' which means that latent power in a person which impels him to do a work. In brief, motivation is that process wherein the persons are made to realise their needs for the realization of which they will do some work for the interests of the enterprise.

Many scholars have given different definitions on the basis of their experience. Some are the following:

According to *Michael J. Jucius,* "Motivation is the act of stimulating someone or oneself to get a desired course of action or to push the right button to get a desired reaction."

According to *Dalton E. McFarland.* "The concept of motivation is mainly psychological. It relates to those forces operating within the individual employee or subordinate which impel him to act or not to act in certain ways."

According to *Koontz and O'Donnell,* "To motivate is to induce people to act in a desired manner.

According to *W.G. Scott,* "Motivation means a process of stimulating people to action to accomplish desired goals."

Characteristics of Motivation

On the basis of the definition the following characteristics of motivation can be placed as:

1. *Motivation is an Internal Feeling.* Motivation is a psychological feeling which lies inward. First of all some needs are felt which affect the behaviour of a person, he thinks of doing some work to satisfy those needs.

2. *Each Person has Different Motivational Factor.* Everybody has different aspirations. Motivational factors happen to be different because of the different needs of different persons.

3. *Motivation is a Continuous Process.* It is a continuous process. The job of a manager does not end by motivating an individual once but he has to be made to realise time and again 'about his needs by way of motivation.

4. *Motivation an Important Function of Management.* Motivation is an important function of management, a manager is not efficient, the manager has made good plans for the achievement of objectives but if does not succeed in motivating the employee to give practical shape to his plans, his effort goes waste.

5. *Different Ways of Motivations.* An important characteristics of motivation is that it can be in many forms. Keeping in view the needs of the people concerned monetary and non-monetary methods of motivation.

6. *It Stimulates People to do Work.* A person is appointed on the basis of his educational qualifications but it is not essential that he works with his full capacity. Motivation stimulates him to do work with his full available ability.

7. *Motivation Creates Morale.* Morale is created among the people by motivating them which converts their ability to do the work into their willingness to do the work. Thus, it is clear that motivation creates morale.

8. *It's Helpful in Securing Industrial Peace.* Apart from motivating people to do their work, motivation helps in securing industrial peace. Motivation helps the people to utilise their full capability which results in good and increased production. The enterprise earns profits and the employees get many facilities. As a result of this both the employer and the employees get satisfaction.

9. *Motivation is Useful for Problem Solving.* The manager is faced with the problem of getting work done by subordinates by making them willing to work. This can only be done with the help of motivation.

10. *It Relates with Human.* Motivation is related with the human. Motivation of human factor automatically leads to the efficient utilization of other non-human factors.

Importance of Motivation

Motivation is an important factor in determining the efficiency of an organization, it develops a desire in the minds of the employees to achieve successfully the objectives of the enterprise. An enterprise may have the best of material, machines and other means of production but all these resources are meaningless so long as they are not utilized by properly motivated people. There was a time when the human resource of production was treated like other non-human resources and was not given any special importance. The old concept has lost all importance in this competitive age. Clarifying the importance of motivation. Allen has stressed the importance and need of motivation by saying; "Poorly motivated people can nullify the soundest organization."

The importance or need of motivation is stressed as:

1. *High Level of Performance.* The efficiency of the motivated employees is better than the unmotivated people. It is important to achieve high level of efficiency can be achieved

through motivation. Researchers have proved the high degree of positive correlation between motivation and efficiency.

2. *Organizational Changes.* Changes take place in the organization like technical changes, methods of work performance, etc. Generally, the employees do not accept changes in the method of work performance they are accustomed. Sometimes changes become necessary keeping in view the demands of time, these changes can be made acceptable through motivation.

3. *Low Employees Turnover and Absenteeism.* The goodwill of an enterprise is adversely affected by the high level of employees turnover and absenteeism. This creates many problems for the managers. The problems of appointing the employees time and again, arranging for their education and training, etc., lead to wastage of time as well as money, motivation can save this wastage for the organization. Motivated people work for a longer time in the enterprise and the rate of absenteeism comes down.

4. *Good Human Relations.* A high level of motivation establishes good relations among the capital and the employees. Motivation fills the employees with enthusiasm and they start accepting orders and information willingly. Motivation makes a great contribution in establishing good human relations.

5. *Good Image of Organization.* Where the employees are motivated through a proper method by satisfying their needs, good image of the enterprise is created in the mind of the public. Qualified employees give preference to seek appointment in such enterprises as the work culture is refined in such organizations.

6. *Increase in Morale.* High level of motivation increases the morale of the employees are not afraid of taking bold decisions as and when need so arise.

7. *Helpful in Achieving Goals.* Motivation is useful in achieving organizational goals in an efficient way as it results in a positive check on all types of wastes.

8. *Proper Use of Human Resources.* Human resource has an important place among the resources of production. The success or failure of an enterprise depends on the proper use of human resource. Its proper use can be made with the help of various types of motivation. Motivated employees work at their full capacity as their aim is achieve the objectives of the enterprise.

The above review makes it clear that motivation is an important tool in the hands of management for the attainment of objectives of the individustrial and the organization economically and effectively. Motivation can be used for improving the qualities of subordinates and control on wastages.

Objectives of Motivation

Motivation is an important function of enlightened management. The objectives of motivation can be highlighted from the description of importance and need discussed in this chapter.

The following are the objectives of motivation:

1. To attain a high level of efficiency.
2. To reduce employees turnover and absenteeism.
3. To make organizational changes acceptable.
4. To establish good relations among the employer and the employees.
5. To create good image of organization.
6. To achieve the goals of the organization.

7. To increase the morale of the employees.
8. To satisfy various needs of the employees.
9. To make proper use of human resources.

Process of Motivation

The process of motivation means an attempt to know from where it starts and where it ends. The work of motivation is completed by many steps. Koontz and O'Donnell have shown the process of motivation as "Needs-Gap-Satisfaction" chain in the following way:

Needs → Give rise to → Wants → Which cause → Tensions
→ Which give rise to → Actions → Which result in → Satisfaction

"Need → Gap → Satisfaction" Chain

In first stage a man feels the need of something, a desire is born in his mind. When a need becomes powerful it gets changed into a want which means that he starts feeling that it should be satisfied. When thoughts come to his mind, tension takes place which makes him tense. The only way to get rid of tension is to do some work. Hence, the situation of action is created. When a man acts to remove the tension created by his needs which has turned itself into a want, he feels satisfaction.

Employees are made to realise their needs through motivation and a feeling to achieve them is born in their mind. The managers make available all the facilities for work performance and, finally, the employees achieve their objective by satisfying their needs. After one need is satisfied, the other is born and the chain continues. It must be made clear that the objective of motivation is not only to satisfy the needs of the employees but to achieve successfully the objectives of the organization.

THEORIES OF MOTIVATION

Motivation is defined by different scholars in different way. The oldest concept is known as 'Carrot and Stick' policy. It means that those employees who work enthusiastically and afficiently are rewarded for their efficiency and those whose work performance is careless are punished. Frederick Taylor, the father of scientific management has advocated a 'incentive remuneration system' of motivation, which means more work should bring more remuneration and little work should bring less remuneration for the employees. However, modern thinkers have amended these old concepts and presented new ideas in this context. These modern theories include Maslow's Need Hierarchy Theory. Herzberg's Motivation-Hygiene Theory, McGregor's X and Y theory, etc. From the point of view of convenience in study the theories about motivation have been divided into two parts. (A) Traditional Theories and (B) Modern Theories.

A. Traditional Theories

1. *Fear and Punishment Theory.* This theory stress on 'fear' has been treated as a proper medium of motivating the employees. The supporters of this theory, the managers should know the weakness of the subordinates. It means that a sense of fear should be created in the mind of the subordinates that if they do not work at their full capability they will be removed from their job. The fear of being removed from their job will keep them frightened and they will work at their full capability.

This concept is like a very strict order and nobody has any alternative except to obey the order. The slogan of this theory is "Either do work or go" and another slogan of this concept is, "Neither make reply or reason why, but to do or die."

Criticism. There are some scholars who support this theory and they think that the principle of motivation can get quick work performance. But in reality this principle is not appropriate in the changing circumstances when the labour unions have come into existence and the workers have become conscious about their rights. Most of the scholars feel that a constant threat of fear weakens the efficiency of the employees. The aim of motivation is defeated.

Utility. This theory was useful when the workers were not united, sources of employment were scarce and labour unions had not come into existence. That was the time of the beginning of the Industrial Revolution, when it was absolutely imperative for the workers to keep alive their source of income and, therefore, they felt motivated by this principle but in the modern times this principle is absolutely unsuccessful.

2. *Reward Theory.* According to this theory man works only to increase his financial profits. It means the more remuneration will result in more work. Thus, if the remuneration is related to the amount of work, the subordinates will put in more hard work. The subordinates will make maximum use of their available capacity to work with a view to get more remuneration. According to this thought the workers work efficiently so long as they get proper reward, meaning thereby that they should be given more salary to get more work. Consequently, they will like to work in the enterprise for a long time. There are two positive effects of this. Firstly, the labour turnover of the enterprise falls which means that the people do not leave the enterprise very soon, and secondly, the people from outside the enterprise also get impressed by the more salary and good work environment. This theory will make help in making good team work.

Criticism. Some scholars look upon this principle with an eye of doubt. They think that man is not an economic being (does not live for earning money) but alongwith economic reward he needs self satisfaction, social prestige, etc. Some researchers feel that money only gives economic satisfaction but not motivation. In this context Peter Drucker feels that, "Satisfaction with monetary rewards is not a sufficient motivator for employees".

Utility. No doubt there are criticism of this theory yet it cannot be denied that remuneration is still the chief attraction for most of the people, meaning thereby that money alone works as a sort of motivation. Monetary reward is important because of the following reasons:

(i) Money alone can be the impartial measurement of the efficiency of different employees. If some more efficient employee is given some facilities instead of money, it does not have any applicable effect on him.

(ii) Reward is a motivating factor because it can easily be increased or decreased according to the proportion of work.

(iii) More salary helps in maintaining economic security, honour and prestige. For example, an employee who used to maintain a bicycle starts maintaining a scooter after getting more salary which increases his prestige.

(iv) Finally, financial incentive creates self-confidence in an employee and encourages him to improve his standard of living.

3. *Carrot and Stick Theory.* According to this theory the employees should be rewarded or punished depending upon the extent of their efficiency. The result is that they are inspired to do more work. Under this the normal work of each employee is determined. If an employee puts in more than his normal work, he should be rewarded and if he performs less work than the normal work he should be punished. According to this theory the reward or more

remuneration than the normal will be given only when the minimum work conditions are satisfied. Many researchers have given their opinions in favour of this theory. According to them by implementing a simultaneous policy of reward and punishment the employees can be motivated.

Criticism. According to scholars the motivation done according to this theory is not successful. According to Bernard, Remuneration more than the normal cannot motivate those who have already got sufficient resurces available to them.

Utility. This theory is more useful when the physical and security needs still remain to be realized. In other words, so long as the employee does not have all the resources at his command, this principle continues motivating him and becomes ineffective after that.

Causes of Failure of Traditional Theories. All the three traditional theories are based on the same pattern. They think that the workers are lazy by nature and they shirk work. Most of the people are afraid of taking any responsibility in the enterprise. They must be pressurised in order to get work out of them and they should be kept under fear. McGregor feels that this concept is based on absolutely false notions. Therefore, in order to utilize the maximum capability of the workers it is not necessary to pressurise them, pay them more remuneration or give punishment but an environment should be created so that the workers willingly move ahead and work. Hence, creating a work conducive environment ainounts to motivating the employees.

B. Modern Theories

The meaning of motivation according to the modern theories is absolutely different from the traditional theories. Traditional theories are based on the concept of getting work out of the employees under threat or fear of pressure because they are shirkers by nature. The modern theories, however, think that the subordinates should be motivated by giving them more responsibility and more authority. It means that the managers far from using unnecessary pressure on the employees should provide such an environment in which everybody starts working according to his available ability and efforts should continue to increase his capability. Following are the prominent modern theories:

1. *Maslow's Need Hierarchy Theory.* The advocate of this theory is Abraham Maslow who first of all presented the need hierarchy theory of motivation in 1943. Maslow developed the theory of motivation on the basis of a chain or sequence of needs. According to him a man has countless needs and they can be categorised on the basis of priority. For example, the needs which are more sharply felt should be satisfied first and the less sharply felt needs should be satisfied afterwards and similarly, the least felt needs should be thought of last of all. Maslow has divided different human needs on. the basis of priority into five parts which are:

(i) Physiological Needs. This category includes those needs which a man needs to satisfy first of all in order to remain alive. It includes food to eat, house to live in, clothes to wear and sleep for rest.

(ii) Safety Needs. After having satisfied the physical needs a man thinks of his safety. Safety needs mean physical, economic and psychological safety. Physical safety means saving him from accidents, attacks, diseases and other unforseen situations. Economic safety means security of employment and making provision for old age. Psychological safety means maintaining his prestige.

(iii) Sodal Needs. Man is a social being and wants to live in society with honour. It is, therefore, necessary that he should have friends and relatives with whom he can share his joys and sorrows. Maslow has placed these needs at the third place.

(iv) Esteem and Status Needs. They are called ego needs of man. It means everybody wants to get a high status which may increase his power and authority.

(v) Self-Actualization Needs. Last of all man tries to satisty his self-actualization need. It means that a man should become what he is capable of. For example, a musician wants to be proficient in the art of music, an artist wants to gain proficiency in creating works of art and similarly, a poet wants to be an expert in the art of writing poems.

The above study shows that a man has various needs and their order can be determined. The moment the first need of man is satisfied he starts thinking of the second need, and then follows his worry about the third need and this sequence continues till all the needs are satisfied. It is thus clear that the needs of a human being serve as a motivation for him. In other words, man starts working at his full capacity in order to satisfy his various needs.

In brief the following facts come to light as a result of Maslow's ideas about motivation:

(i) Man does every work in order to satisfy his need.

(ii) These needs can be divided into five parts.

(iii) The order of priority of these needs can be determined which is not permanent. Different people can have different order of priorities.

(iv) When all the needs of a man remain unrealized, his first need is a sort of motivation for him. As soon as his need is satisfied his motivation ends, as for as the first need is concerned and in that case his second need becomes his motivating factor. In this way the chain of needs continues and man himself remains motivated.

Criticism. If no special study is made Maslow's need hierarchy theory appears to be appropriate but various researchers have given their opinion against this theory. Their criticism is as follows:

(i) The chain of need hierarchy theory of Maslow is not permanent. This undergoes changes according to the situations.

(ii) This is not necessary that the needs of one category may be stronger at a time and the other remain unimportant.

2. *Herzberg's Motivation-Hygiene Theory.* This theory has been advocated by Prof. Herzberg on the basis of his research done in collaboration with his colleagues. After interviewing some employees he concluded that motivating factors can be divided into two parts.

(a) Maintenance or Hygiene or Dissatisfiers. Maintenance factors mean those factors whose presence does not motivate the employees to work with greater enthusiasm but their absence does discourage them. These factors are related to the job conditions and they contain the following factors:

(i) Company's Policy and Administration,

(ii) Technical Inspection,

(iii) Mutual Personal Relation with Inspector,

(iv) Mutual Relation with other Team Managers,

(v) Salary,

(vi) Working Conditions,

(vii) Personal Life,

(viii) Security of Employment,

(ix) Status, and

(x) Environment.

(b) Motivators or Satisfiers. Motivating factors mean those factors which directly inspire the employees to work. These factors are directly related to work and they are also known as job factors. These are as follows:

(i) Achievement,

(ii) Recognition,

(iii) Advancement,

(iv) Job itself,

(v) Opportunities for Growth, and

(vi) Responsibility.

According to Herzberg the employees remain satisfied with the available maintenance factors and do not get motivated by any increase in them. They, however, get dissatisfied by their decrease. For example, if an employee is taken out of a working group whom he likes and is placed in another working group, his enthusiasm will decline, while an additional person of the same type in the same group will not boost his enthusiansm. On the other hand, motivating factors directly affect the enthusiasm of the employees, meaning thereby any addition in them increases their enthusiasm and any decrease lessens it. For example, an employee of some department who is declared the best worker on the basis of his efficiency will make him work with greater efficiency.

Criticism. Like other theories this theory is also not free from criticism. Scholars have criticised this theory on the basis of the following facts:

(i) The maintenance factors pointed out by Herzberg are not appropriate in all the situations. For example, an increase in pay does not mean an increase in the enthusiasm of the employees but this is applicable only in those countries where a guarantee for average

living standard is held out. In other words, where the government assures a general living standard as an essential guarantee, an increase in salary becomes meaningless. On the other hand, it has been established on the basis of various researches that in the undeveloped countries rise in salary does create enthusiasm among the employees.

(ii) The categorization of dissatisfiers and satisfiers is not practical.

(iii) This theory has made the relationship between motivation and satisfaction very simple when it is not so.

In short, it can be said that alongwith the satisfiers the dissatisfiers also increase the enthusiasm of the employees.

3. McGregor's X and Y Theory. Douglas McGregor has presented the traditional concept of motivation as the X theory and the modern concept as Y theory. Following are the assumptions of both these theories:

Traditional Theory 'X'	*Modern Theory 'Y'*
1. Man by nature is sluggish and shirker.	1. Man wants to work provided the conditions are favourable.
2. Mostly people are not ambitious and are afraid to make responsibility.	2. This theory takes people as enthusiastic responsible, and full of effort.
3. Under this people want to be directed, meaning thereby that they want somebody to tell them to work and only then they will work.	3. It is thought that the employee has the quality of self-direction and they do not feel the necessity of being directed by somebody else.
4. Motivation is limited to only physical and security needs.	4. According to this, physical and security needs motivate for a short time while it is continuous in case of self-actualization, and esteem and status needs.

According to McGregor the managers supporting 'X' theory (who consider employees lazy, selfish, unambitious, opponents of changes) employ punishment, threat, strict inspection, etc., as methods of getting work but this arrangement is never successful because the use of force gives rise to opposition, encouragement to trade unions, puts hindrance in production, and finally the attainment of managerial objectives become difficult. McGregor suggests that such managers should not use pressure tactics and should try to win over the employees with a soft attitude.

On the contrary, the managers who support the 'Y' theory think that the employees are enthusiastic and ambitious. That is why these managers believe in giving more freedom and responsibility to them. In conclusion it can be said that McGregor is of the opinion that the employees should be motivated by making use of decentralization, and a system of participation and consultation. By doing so the employees will work willingly and feel motivated for self appraisal of their responsibility.

Principles of Motivations

The importance of motivation in an organization cannot be under estimated, it is essential to launch a successful motivation movement in order to attain success in the objectives of the organization. Motivation movement can be made success only if it is implemented on the basis of certain principles. The main principles of motivation are as follows:

1. Principle of work appreciation.
2. Principle of making work interesting.
3. Principle of team spirit.
4. Principle of recognition of employees.
5. Principle of work security.

6. Principle of security against accident.
7. Principle of leadership.
8. Principle of capability.
9. Principle of incentives.
10. Principle of division of work.

Technique of Motivation

Motivation can bring out the latent capabilities of people, how it should be done? As people have different nature and it is quite possible that one factor of motivation may be successful in motivating a particular person while the same factor may not be successful in case of another person. Even then there can be some general factors which may affect most of the people. Motivation techniques are known as types, kinds, methods, classification and tools. The main techniques of motivation are as under:

1. Positive and Negative Motivation

(a) Positive Motivation. Positive motivation means that motivation with which the employees are motivated in respect of their work by offering them some economic incentive. According to Flippo, "Positive motivation is a process of attempting to influence others to do their work through the possibility of gain or reward." According to Flippo the following techniques of motivation can prove to be positive:

(i) To give suggestion about new work.

(ii) To give information.

(iii) To arrange competitions from time to time.

(iv) Managers should take personal interest in the subordinates capabilities development.

(v) To create an inclination to accept responsibility.

(vi) To make them feel the pride or being a part of the enterprise.

(vii) To increase subordinate importance by giving them participation in management.

(viii) to increase salary.

The feeling of confidence and belongingness towards the enterprise can be created among the employees through positive motivation. Consequently, available capability will be fully utilized for the benefit of the enterprise.

(b) Negative Motivation. Negative motivation means which is sought to be created by the managers by resorting to threat, punishment or fear and get the work done according to their wishes. This may be useful for it short period but has disastrous consequences in the long run. Likert has pointed out in this context that, "In the long run negative motivation reduces the productivity." Following are the chief examples of negative motivation:

(i) Frightening them.

(ii) Criticizing them.

(iii) Threatening removal from service.

(iv) Taking penal action.

(v) Ignoring and treating them cruelly.

2. Financial and Non-Financial Motivation

(a) Financial Motivation. Financial motivations are those motivations which are evaluated in terms of money. Evaluation in terms of money does not mean that all types of motivation should be in the form of money but some such facilities can be provided as can be evaluated in terms of money. For example, rent free house, car, facility of a servant, etc. Following can be included among the chief financial motivation.

(i) Increase in salary or wages.

(ii) Giving bonus (a share in the profits of the enterprise).

(iii) Premium (a share of profit due to increased production because of the employees' effort).

(iv) Retirement benefits.

(v) Free insurance facility.

(vi) Commission.

(vii) Salary for leave.

(viii) Free medical treatment facility.

There are different opinions regarding the success of financial factors of motivation. According to one opinion these incentives are most successful because everybody gets satisfied by more money. More money in itself is an indication of status. In this context Flippo has said that, "man gets motivated by the satisfaction of other needs with money." On the other hand, some people have an opposite opinion. They think that money is not everything, man has a desire to have social respect and status. It is not necessary that money may bring respect. For example, one can have more money by working in an ill-reputed concern but not respect. Even then we can say in conclusion that financial gain is the best source of motivation.

(b) Non-Financial Motivation. Non-Financial motivation is not directly related with money. These motivations help in the satisfaction of top hierarchy needs like respect, self-actualization, etc. They are related with the internal feelings of the employees, meaning there by that these are psychological motivators. According to Dubin, "Non-financial motivations are in the form of mental reward". In the opinion of Chester Bernard, "It is a common feeling that material reward (like money) becomes ineffective after a certain

extent." It means that non-financial rewards are more effective than the financial rewards in order to motivate materially prosperous persons. The following factors are primarily helpful in motivating the employees with non-financial rewards:

(i) *Job Security.* Job security is an important non-financial motivating factor. Job security implies permanence of employment. For example, if a man is afraid of the fact that he can be removed from his job any time he will not work with his heart and soul and its worry keeps him upset.

(ii) *Opportunities of Promotion.* The employees working in the enterprise know that by displaying better efficiency they can achieve high post, the desire for high post motivates them. Consequently, they have no stone unturned in-utilizing their capability. When a clerk clearly visualize that there is no possibility of his promotion and he will continue working on the same post, his working will comparatively be slow.

(iii) *Praise.* "Everybody wants his work to be appreciated and he be respected as a human being." It means that the efficiency of any person can be increased to a large extent by appreciating his work. Hence, good effort made by the employees should be appreciated.

(iv) *Employees Participation in Management.* Employees and workers get motivated when seeing their participate in management. they offer full cooperation in making the policies and work with utmost care.

(v) *Individual Recognition.* Everybody wants to be recognised as an important part of the enterprise. Managers should so divide the work among the employees as to give an impression to everybody that a particular work depends on him alone. By getting this importance they start working more laboriously and responsibly.

(vi) *Good Leadership.* People working on high posts in the enterprise possess qualities of an efficient leadership, the subordinates get motivated because an efficient leader can easily understand their feelings and does not allow any unwanted problem to crop up.

(vii) *Guarantee of Justice.* When all the employees working in the enterprise are treated equally and everybody gets justice. No step-motherly treatment, work more efficiently, the managers should pay equal salary and other facilities for equal work.

(viii) *Knowledge of Secret Information.* All the people working in the enterprise have a curiosity to know about the progress of the enterprise and its future plans. Therefore, the managers should inform the subordinates from time to time about the progress of the enterprise and the future plans. This creates a sense of belongingness towards the enterprise.

(ix) *Delegation of Authority.* Delegation of authority means that the subordinates should given authority alongwith the assignment of work. By such an arrangement they come to realize the responsibilities connected with their post. They, therefore, work with more alertness and become more experienced.

(x) *Constructive Attitude.* Most of the people have a constructive attitude. If the managers afford an opportunity to the employees to freely display their knowledge and proficiency, the employees will be motivated and the enterprise, in turn, will be benefited more.

(xi) *Fearless Environment.* Employees can be motivated by providing a fearless environment to them. More work can be extracted out of the employees under pressure or by frightening them only for a short span of time, but in the long run their capability is adversely affected. Troubled by such an atmosphere efficient employees leave the enterprise and the remaining ones do not put their heart and soul into their work. Consequently, production in the enterprise decreases. Therefore, the manager should create a friendly environment instead of fear.

(xii) *Job Rotation and Alteration.* Some enterprises motivate their employees by making use of job rotation. Under this method the employees are given an opportunity from time to time to work according to their ability on all the available posts for some time. This change can put an end to the feelings of disinterestedness in doing the same work again and again. Another benefit of this method is that it increases the knowledge of the employees.

3. Individual and Group Motivation

(a) Individual Motivation. Under individual motivation an employee is individually motivated to inspire him more towards his work. This motivation can both be financial and non-financial. This mostly includes appreciation letters, opportunities for development, security of employment, rise in salary, etc. In any work in the enterprise which can be idividually evaluated, these motivations should be adopted by doing so the employee comes to know about his efficiency and he tries to work more efficiently.

Advantages of Individual Motivation. Individual motivations given to the employees in an enterprise have the following advantages:

(i) These motivations have a good effect on the comparatively less efficient employees. The rewards

given to their colleagues increase their desire which makes them put in more efforts in their work.

(ii) Those employees who get individual regards start working with greater efficiency.

(iii) Individual motivation indicates respect. This gives the employee a sense of prestige.

(iv) The manager's job of evaluation becomes simple because the assessment of an individual's work is easier.

(v) The efficient employee from outside gets attracted by the individual encouragement given to the employees in an enterprise.

(b) Group Motivation. Group motivation is related to a group rather than a particular individual. These motivations can also be financial as well non-financial. These include giving a particular part of the profits of the enterprise to all the employees, awarding a shield or trophy to the employees of some department for their efficiency, getting cooperation of all the employees of a group in the solution of a particular problem, distribution of bonus among all the employees, etc. To understand both the types of motivation the example of a cricket match can be helpful. In a cricket match the victorious team usually gets two prizes—firstly, the man of the match which is an individual motivation, and secondly, a trophy which is a group motivation.

Advantages of Group Motivation. Following are the advantages of group motivation:

(i) This motivation checks the feeling of mutual conflict or difference of opinion among the different employees in a group.

(ii) There is not much need of inspecting the employees because all work with a team spirit.

(iii) These motivations establish industrial peace.

(iv) When a work is to be performed by a team, no employee shows carelessness and all, remain present at the right time. Consequently, more work becomes possible in less time and at a less cost.

(v) Group motivation raises the reputation of the enterprise in the eyes of the outsiders.

4. Extrinsic and Intrinsic Motivation

(a) Extrinsic Motivation. Extrinsic motivators are those motivators which impress the employees while working but they get them only afterwards. For example, the retirement plans formulated by the employers for the welfare of the employees. The benefit of these plans is received by the employees only after retirement but they affect their efficiency right from the day one. They mostly include rise in salary, life insurance, arrangement for resting after work, leaves, etc.

(b) Intrinsic Motivation. Intrinsic motivators are those motivators in whose case the time of their receipt by the employees and the effect on their efficiency happens to be the same. It means that as they keep on getting them, their efficiency keeps on increasing. For example, when an employee is given the feeling that he happens to be an important part of the enterprise, meaning thereby that his identity has been established, this immediately affects his efficiency. This includes respect, responsibility and participation These. motivations are generally non-monetary.

Essentials of a Successful Motivational System

After having studied the various methods of motivation in detail it is clear that all of them have their own merits and limitations. A particular system may be beneficial in a particular situation while some other may be useful in another situation. Koontz and O'Donnell says a successful system of motivation must have the followjng four essential qualities.

1. *Productive.* The first essential of a successful motivational system is to implement such a system as to increase the efficiency of the subordinates.

2. *Comprehensive.* A system of motivation will be considered good if it has the quality of being comprehensive. Comprehensiveness can be considered in two ways, firstly, a system will be called comprehensive which is applicable, equally to all the employees, and secondly, a system which satisfies all the top and low hierarchy needs of the employees.

3. *Competitive.* The motivational system should create a spirit of competition among the employees so that everybody tries to put in his best effort for the attainment of pre-determined objectives. For example, while determining the time and quality of work, it is done in lesser time if provision of reward is made. All the employees will work with a competitive spirit to get the prize, as a result of this their efficiency will increase.

4. *Flexible.* The system of motivation should be flexible so that it can be charged easily in times of need without any opposition.

Apart from the above there are many other important facts which affect the success of a motivational system. These are as follows:

(i) *Easily Understandable.* Motivational system should be easily understandable to all the employees and workers of all the levels whether educated or uneducated.

(ii) *Regular Motivation.* Motivational system should provide regular motivation to the employees. It should not be such which provides motivation for a short span of time but should motivate the employees of the enterprise.

(iii) *Easy Implementation.* Motivational system should have the quality of easy implementation.

(iv) *Increase in Reputation.* Motivational system should be able to increase the reputation of both the enterprise and the employees.

(v) *Based on Organizational Goals.* Motivational system should be directly linked with the goals of the enterprise. The system should be designed to achieve easily the pre-determined objectives of the enterprise.

(vi) *Justifiable.* The motivational system should be justifiable which means that there should be equal reward for equal achievement.

(vii) *Based on Standards.* Standards signify the work expected of the subordinates so that the reward can be determined by comparing the standard work with the actual performance.

(viii) *Based on Principles.* Motivational system should be based on some basic principles. The one principle of motivation is 'human behaviour' and, therefore, the system should be based on the principle of human behaviour.

The above analysis makes it clear that a manager should pay special attention to these facts while choosing a successful motivational system.

Problems or Hurdles in Motivation

Motivation is the outcome of a certain relation between the superiors and the subordinates. For this the superiors or the managers make special efforts different from the daily control or functions. It is not necessary that the efforts made by the managers will be unanimously acceptable. It can also be opposed. In this way there are many hurdles in implementing a motivational systems. They are as follows:

1. *A Costly Effort.* A major aim of implementing a motivational system is to raise the efficiency of the employees. If the labour put in its implementation becomes successful, it is not at all costly. It is, however, often seen that even after making all efforts the expected level of efficiency is not attained. In such a situation it proves to be a costly process.

2. *Motivation is an Internal Feeling.* Generally, it is understood that motivation is an inner feeling of man. This feeling cannot be had by giving some order or be inspired by implementing any plan. So long as the employee does not have an urge to work from within all efforts come to naught. For example, those people who have the inner urge to work, they do not need any motivation. On the other hand, those who lack this urge cannot be motivated by any number of efforts.

3. *Opposition to Changes.* Human nature does not accept changes easily. People get accustomed to the system in vogue and want to work within that system. Therefore, whenever some new plan is implemented they oppose it aod become a hindrance in its success.

4. *Trouble Making Employees.* In every enterprise there are some troublesome employees. Their only purpose is to create trouble and not to allow the policies to be implemented. The problems of such employees are altogether different and serious. It is a tough job to motivate them. Therefore, these people can be a hindrance in the implementation of any motivational plan.

In this way there are many opposing factors which make efforts to make motivational system unsuccessful. But a successful manager faces these hurdles dauntlessly and achieves his objective.

❋❋❋

11

ENTREPRENEURIAL DEVELOPMENT PROGRAMME

Entrepreneurial Development Programme (EDP) designed to help a person in strengthening and fulfilling his entrepreneurial motive and in acquiring skills and capabilities necessary for playing his entrepreneurial role effectively. Towards this end, it is necessary to promote his understanding of motives, motivation pattern, their impact on behaviour and entrepreneurial value. A programme which seeks to do this can qualify to be called a programmer. This has to be stressed here, because there are a number of programmes which aim at providing informational or managerial inputs or focus on preparation of a project. EDP has been recognized as an effective human resource development tool, many a times there are very many expectations from a single programme, like removing unemployment, enhancing industrial development, promoting small-scale industries, developing industrially underdeveloped regions, etc.

EDP is primarily meant for developing these first-generation entrepreneurs, who on their own cannot become successful entrepreneurs. It covers three major variables: location, target group and enterprise (entrepreneurial activities). Any of these can become the focus or starting point for initiating and implementing an EDP.

Entrepreneurship Development Programme (EDP)

In the recent years EDP package, have become a vital strategy for harnessing the vast untapped human skills, to use these for converting into industrialization entrepreneurship development has become extremely important in achieving the goals of all-around development in the country. Consequently, many entrepreneurial opportunities are emerging in various fields. Be it electronic, medicine, engineering, agriculture, communication, atomic energy, telecommunication, food technology and packaging, entrepreneurial opportunities have swfaced at rapid pace in all these and many other areas. Such opportunities, however, become more perceptible and profitable to entrepreneurs when exposed to latest developments in the respective fields either in terms of technology, use or style of living. Accessibility and understanding of such information widens the base of opportunity sensing by potential entrepreneurs.

Objectives of the EDP

The EDP was considered a part of the industrial development policy which was articulated in the Five-Year National Economic and Social development Plan. The Programme had sought to develop entrepreneurial activities in the rural areas of many countries as a vehicle for economic growth with the achievement of the following are the objectives of EDP.

(a) To promote the development of small and medium enterprises that would encourage self-employment among potential entrepreneurs;

(b) To generate employment and self-employment opportunities in the processing of indigenous raw materials for local consumption and for export;

(c) To provide, in the rural areas, special programmes designed to stimulate new ventures and encourage expansion of existing activities of small and medium industries;

(d) To develop entrepreneurial opportunities for potential entrepreneurs and upgrade managerial skills for existing entrepreneurs.

For a sound training programme for entrepreneurship development in India, the expert group constituted by the NIESBUD accepted that it must be able to help selected entrepreneurs to:

(a) Develop and strengthen their entrepreneurial quality/motivation;

(b) Analyse environment related to small industry and small business;

(c) Select project/product;

(d) Formulate projects;

(e) Understand the process and procedure of setting up of small enterprise;

(f) Acquire the basic management skills;

(g) Know the pros and cons of being an entrepreneur;

(h) Know and influence the source of help/support needed for launching the enterprise;

(i) Acquaint and appreciate the needed social responsibility/entrepreneurial disciplines.

Some of the other important objectives of entrepreneurial training are:

(i) To let the entrepreneur set or reset the objectives of his business and work individually and along with his group for their realization.

(ii) To enable him to take strategic decisions.

(iii) To prepare him for accepting totally unforeseen risks of business after such training.

(iv) To enable him to build an integrated team to fulfil the demands of tomorrow.

(v) To communicate fast, clearly and effectively.

(vi) To enable him to cope with and coordinate all relevant paper work, most of which is statutorily obligatory.

(vii) To develop a broad vision to see the business as a whole and to integrate his function with it.

(viii) To strengthen his integrity, honesty, and compliance with law, the key to success in the long run.

(ix) To make him accept industrial democracy, that is, accepting workers as partners in enterprise.

Evolution of Entrepreneurship Development Programmes

The various motivation campaigns or programmes taken up by the Small Industries Service Institute and SIET Institute in the sixties tried to fill the existing information gaps relevant for small entrepreneurs. The entrepreneurs required a lot of information and technological know-how for setting up a business and in that context, the contribution of these programmes was essentially in the area of disseminating knowledge on financial, technical and managerial aspects. To that extent, these programmes were in the nature of supportive programmes for the existing and new entrepreneurs.

Based on the above experience and in the context of the emergence of financial and industrial development corporations in the states, it was visualized that creation of all external facilities is not a sufficient condition for the promotion of entrepreneurship. Equally important are qualities of the individual who responds to the external opportunities (*i.e.*, availability of funds, financial incentives, etc.) Also, social and organizational factors help people to perceive opportunities and learn to respond to them.

1. Entrepreneurial education.
2. Planned publicity for entrepreneurial opportunities.
3. Identification of potential entrepreneurs through scientific method.
4. Motivational training to new entrepreneurs.
5. Help and guidance in selecting products and preparing project reports.
6. Making available techno-economic information and product profits.
7. Evolving locally suitable new products and processes.
8. Availability of local agencies with trained personnel for entrepreneurial counselling and promotions.
9. Creating entrepreneurial forum.
10. Recognition of entrepreneurial skills.

Entrepreneurial Development Cycle

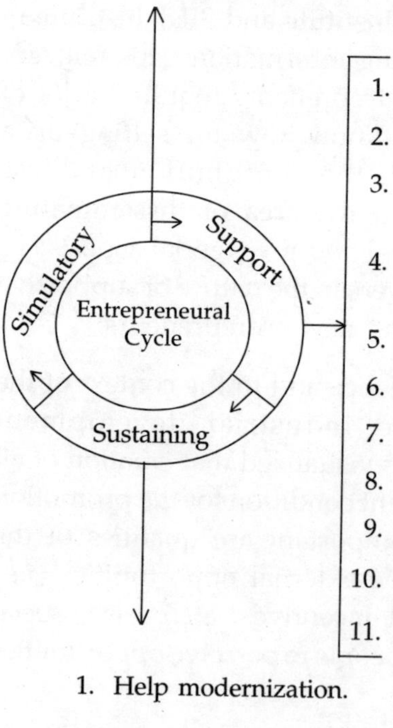

1. Registration of unit.
2. Arranging finance.
3. Providing land, shed, power, water, etc.
4. Guidance for selecting and obtaining machinery.
5. Supply of scarce raw materials.
6. Getting licences/import licences.
7. Providing common facilities.
8. Granting tax relief or other subsidy.
9. Offering management consultancy.
10. Help marketing product.
11. Providing information.

1. Help modernization.

2. Help diversification/expansion/substitute production.
3. Additional financing for full capacity utilization.
4. Deferring repayment/interest.
5. Diagnostic industrial extension/consultancy source.
6. Production units legislation/policy change.
7. Product reservation/creating new avenues for marketing.
8. Quality testing and improving services.
9. Need-based common facilities centre.

Increasing Importance of EDP. The development of EDP as a strategy contributing to the industrialization and economic growth of backward and other areas needs a proper direction and organization for making it more effective and purposeful. The contribution of EDPs is very uneven in different regions thus arises the need for a well thought upgradation programme. The important issues to be taken care while applying the EDP are:

1. *Structure of EDP.* The EDP programme should have a practical content with inter-institutional organizational arrangement to make it a success. The successful EDPs have, at their base, the inter-institutional cooperation or an institution such as Gujarat Centre of the State Bank of India, which besides having conducted the programmes has also arranged for finance and other inputs for the entrepreneurs. The EDPs conducted in isolation would dissipate resources and talents. The issue, therefore, for effective functioning of EDPs is to have a financial agency strongly backing up efforts for entrepreneurial development. The place and role of TCOs need to be reviewed and their activities suitably accelerated. Who should conduct an EDP is an important issue.

2. *Areas of Operation of EDP.* As has been stated earlier, in North-Eastern Area, entrepreneurial development activities

have not been benefiting from the support activities of financial institutions. In these areas, programmes have to be linked with support activities.

3. *Fixing Order of Preference.* Another area of fixing the priorities of EDPs is to consider their working in terms of efficiency and social need criteria. Evaluation of EDPs have revealed that those who have business experience, education and skills are providing successful entrepreneurs. This source should be tapped first and then go to the status to cover entrepreneurs from the non-traditional class, *i.e.,* without business and industrial experience, but having the potential of becoming successful entrepreneurs. Next come the entrepreneurs belonging to backward and other communities who have to overcome many additional handicaps to become successful entrepreneurs. A proper course content of EDPs has to be developed to meet the specific requirements of each of these three strata of entrepreneurs in proper balance, without sacrificing the efficiency criteria.

4. *Lack of Specialists' Support.* Entrepreneurship has been an area of study requiring inter-disciplinary efforts by people from different disciplines. A large number of organizations/ agencies engaged in entrepreneurship development in India do not have in the home all the specialists required and have to depend upon outside faculty. The number of specialists available in the country for developing small-scale industries is not very large. As a result, many a time organizations are unable to locate/avail services of experts. On the other hand, there are specialists who have time to spare in which they can render their services to the organizations.

Problems of EDP

ED Programmes in India are afficted with a number of operational problems. As such, though there are many an institution to train entrepreneurs, the growth of erttrepreneurs is inhibited by these problems. The operational problems of EDP are as follows:

1. *Inherent Inability.* There appears to be an inherent inability to identify the needs of the institution and differences of opinion prevailing amongst the practitioners and trainers.

2. *Low Institution Support.* There seems to be low institutional commitment for local support to entrepreneurs besides low involvement of marketing, voluntary and financial institutions in the programme, except for a few.

3. *Non-availability of Raw Materials.* Non-availability of various inputs, *i.e.*, raw materials, power, etc. and infrastructural support entwined with poor follow-up by the primary monitoring institution, results in failure of EDP.

4. *Ill-planned Training Methodology.* There seems to be ill-planned training methodology, inconsistency in programme design, its content, sequence and theme and focus of the programme.

5. *Poor Follow-up.* Training institutions do not show much concern for objective identification and selection of entrepreneurs and the follow-up after training.

6. *Limited Man Power.* Those involved and concerned with the selection and follow-up activities have either limited manpower support or a narrow linkage with other support agencies.

7. *No Clear Cut Course of Action.* There does not appear to be standard course curricula even in terms of broad module being adopted by such institutions.

8. *No Clear Cut Objective.* Majority of the institutions engaged in EDP are themselves not convinced of what they are doing as a task delegated by the Government of helping the policy in attaining its social objectives.

9. *Lack of Creativity and Commitment.* Perceptual ambiguity of the EDP objective seems to have percolated to grassroot level with a significant distortion both in terms of content and intent.

It can be stated that many of the issues related to an EDP are conceptual in nature, many are practical and operational and many are in the borderline between concept and practice. Research and studies, building sophisticated skills and expertise, coordinating, collaborating, corroboration of ideas and actions are necessary strategies that should be continuously pursued to confront these issues.

Entrepreneurship Development Programmes

Major findings with regard to entrepreneurship development programmes are as follows:

Pre-training Promotional Work

One of the important factors in the success of an EDP is considered to be the pretraining promotional work done by the training organization. It was, therefore, planned to identify various activities involved in pre-training promotional work and the extent to which such activities were carried out by training organizations. Based on the information made available by the remaining 19 ED organizations the major activities during pre-training period and the extent to which they were carried out by these organizations have been shown in Table 1 on next page.

It is evident from Table 1. that all those organizations which conducted EDPs gave programme highlighted the programme advertisement in local newspapers. The advertisement highlighted the programme objectives, target group, course contents, eligibility criteria, methodology of conducting the programmes, assistance in project identification and post-training follow-up support. In most cases single advertisement in one of the local newspapers was considered adequate. However, when the course was conducted in smaller towns where availability of adequate number of participants was doubtful the training institutions advertised the programme in more than one newspapers. Programme advertisement was repeated after a gap of 15-20 days if the response was found inadequate. Programme advertisements usually appeared one to two months before start of an EDP.

Second most important pre-training promotional activity was identification of resource persons for conduct of the course. Technical Consultancy Organizations, Small Industries Service Institutes and institutions with limited number of activities considered faculty identification far more important an activity in comparison to education and training institutions. Interaction with education and training institutions revealed that such institutions considered themselves better equipped in terms of faculty resource. Guest faculty in EDPs was usually drawn from engineering colleges, management departments in universities, industry, supporting agencies, banks, corporations, consultancy firms and degree colleges. While the training organizations did not report any problem in getting resource persons in state capitals and places of industrial and commercial importance, availability of faculty did pose a serious problem at district headquarters and small towns.

Table 1

Pre-training Activities and Extent to which they were carried out by ED organizations

Sr. No.	*Activity*	*Carried out by (No. of ED Organizations)*
1.	Programme announcement in local newspapers	19
2.	Identification of faculty for EDPs	10

Contd.

3.	Visits to various organizations by course faculty	9
4.	Programme publicity through supporting organizations	7
5.	Circular letters to various organizations	6
6.	Radio announcements	4
7.	Hand bills and pamphlets	4
8.	Identification of viable venture opportunities	4
9.	Preparation of instructional material	3
10.	Arranging infrastructure for conduct of EDPs	3
11.	Finalising course curriculum	2
12.	Visit to technical institutions and Employment	2
13.	Exchanges visits to industrial areas	1

Source: Compiled from data provided by ED Organizations.

Visit to various organizations and institutions associated with entrepreneurship development was third activity falling under pre-training promotional work. Out of 19 ED organizations nine had reported to have undertaken such activity. This activity was carried out with the twin objectives of generating awareness about the programme and seeking cooperation from such organizations. Majority of the training organizations reported to have received good response from organizations whom they visited.

Out of 19 organizations seven reported that they had requested the supporting institutions to publicize the programmes. Such publicity was usually done by supporting institutions by way of notifying the programme brochures at conspicuous places and circulating the information among officers and staff who matter in such work.

The practice of sending circular letter to various organizations involved in entrepreneurship promotion was found to have been adopted by only six organizations. The purpose of writing such circular letters was to spread message about the programme. Training organizations told that such an attempt helped them in getting better response to the EDPs. Wherever feasible such circular letters were followed up by personal visits by programme coordinator. Radio announcements about the programme were got made by only four ED organizations. Such announcements were made through local/nearest station of All India Radio and contents of radio announcements were largely the same as that of newspaper advertisement. Training institutions did not report any problem in getting such announcements made. The purpose of announcement was to reach EDPs aspirants in far flung areas where newspapers might not be much effective. There were, however, no evidences to conclude effectiveness of such announcements through All India Radio.

Programme advertisement by way of sticking/ distributing hand bills was found to have been practiced by four organizations. Such hand bills usually carried a concise version of programme advertisement. The main objective of hand bills was to supplement the efforts of ED organizations in spreading the message about EDPs. When asked to mention as to how hand bills helped, it was revealed that handbills were usually stuck on local buses, local trains, public places and they were got put on notice boards of educational institutes and agencies assisting entrepreneurs. Two of the organizations got the hand bills inserted in newspapers through hawkers.

Identification of viable venture opportunities in the districts where EDPs were to be conducted was usually insisted upon by the EDPs sponsor as an important pretraining activity. However, this activity was reported to have been carried out by only four out of 19 ED organizations. The purpose of identifying venture opportunities in advance was to help the EDPs participants in identification of projects which suit them. With a view to prepared list of viable projects in the districts the ED organizations visited major industries around, made use of secondary data from various sources and then decided the projects which could be taken up by trainees. The benefit of such an exercise was not found to have reached to those EDPs beneficiaries who expected that such help would be forthcoming during the programme. Table 2 provides us details about the benefit of opportunity identification availed by EDP beneficiaries.

It is evident from Table 2 that most of those who got into an EDP without any project idea failed to finalise projects for themselves by the end of the training programmes. Out of 38 respondents who expected that training institutions will help them in identifying a suitable project, only five could decide the projects during training and six felt to have been assisted to some extent. Remaining 27 respondents could not benefit from opportunity guidance sessions. EDPs participants were asked to mention as to how did they decide the projects for themselves. Participants were of the view that training organizations as well as experts invited to provide opportunity guidance gave very general guidelines' for identification of a suitable project. Specific project ideas which the EDP participants could have thought of implementing, were, by and large, missing. An introspection in present practices of providing opportunity guidance to potential entrepreneurs poses a serious question of as to how opportunity guidance sessions could be made effective.

Table 2

Distribution of EDPs Beneficiaries showing Benefits of Opportunity Guidance

Sr. No.	*Particulars of EDPs Beneficiaries*	*No. of EDP Beneficiaries*
1.	Total No. of sample respondents	127
2.	No. of samples respondents who did not need help in project/product selection	89

Contd.

3.	No. of sample respondents who needed help in project/product selection	38
4.	No. of respondents who got needed help in project/product selection	5
5.	No. of respondents who felt to have been assisted to some extent in project/product selection	6
6.	No. of respondents who needed help in project/product selection and did not get it	27

Source: Compiled from data provided by ED Organizations.

Even though preparation of instructional material was considered an important pretraining activity but it was reported to have been carried out by only three ED organizations. The three organizations included education and training institutions involved in the task of entrepreneurship promotion. Why did other training institutions not carried out this activity before training is something which need to be explored. There could possibly be two reasons for this: *(i)* either the other training institutions had already prepared instructional material for EDPs or *(ii)* they did not consider it an important pre-training activity.

Arranging infrastructure for conduct of EDPs was considered as an exclusive pretraining activity by three ED organizations. These three ED organizations included state level Industrial and Technical Consultancy Organizations which conducted large number of EDPs away from their headquarters. Since other institutions did not conduct EDPS away from their headquarters/branch offices so they might not have considered this activity as part of their pre-programme preparations.

Out of 19 organization two had finalized the course curriculum prior to start of the programme. Others were reported to be doing it on weekly or fortnightly basis. This approach of ED organizations clearly showed *ad-hocism* and lack of standardised approach to programme inputs.

Two organizations visited technical institutions and employment exchanges with a view to spread message about EDPs. Another organization deputed its officers even to an industrial are for the same purpose. To what extent such visits were effective and should such visits be planned as a part of pre-training activity is something which the professionals in the field of entrepreneurship promotion need to look into.

The foregoing discussion has thrown light on various activities involved in pretraining preparations. Release of programmes advertisement in leading local newspaper, identification of resource persons for the course, visit by the programme co-ordinator to various supporting organizations, requesting supporting institutions to publicise the programme, and sending circular letters to organizations which matter constituted important pre-training activities in conduct of EDPs. Radio announcernent, sticking of hand bills, visits to educational institutions and employment exchanges, and visits to industrial areas were also tried to attract applicants. Identificatioi. of viable project ideas, preparation of instructional material and arranging infrastructure for smooth conduct of EDPs were other activities which were required to be taken up before conduct of EDPs. Programme sponsoring organizations while deciding budgets for EDPs may assess the requirement of carrying out such activities and provide needed funds to training organizations.

Process of Selecting Trainees for EDPs

At important aspect of this study was to find out the present practices of selection of entrepreneurs to training programmes. All the 21 entrepreneurship training organizations were requested to provide this information. Interaction with training institutions revealed that selection mechanism was needed for elimination purpose as well as for identification of persons with entrepreneurial trails. On the basis of entrepreneurs identification mechanism the organizations could be categorised as shown in Table 3.

Table 3

Distribution of ED Organizations according to Basis of Selecting EDP Beneficiaries

Sr. No.	*Basis of Selection*	*No. of Organizations*
1.	Application scrutiny, written behavioural test and interview	5
2.	Application scrutiny and performance in interview	13
3.	Application scrutiny, performmance in interview and details of proposed project	1
4.	Non-respondents (*i.e.* EDPs sponsoring organizations)	2
	Total	21

Source: Complied from data provided by Ed Organizations.

It is evident from Table 3 that vast majority of training institutions, *i.e.* 13 out of 19 preferred selecting candidates for the programmes through scrutiny of application black followed by interview. Interaction with training organizations further revealed that no rejection/short listing of candidates took place at application stage. All those who applied for EDPs were interviewed and selection was made based on performance in interview and his/her aptitude for setting up own enterprise. Training institutions also told that it was not the financial background of the candidate which mattered rather it was his/her aptitude and project idea which was given maximum weightage.

The three tier selection mechanism, *i.e.* scrutiny of candidates through application blank followed by written behavioural test and interview was followed by five training organizations. This mechanisms of entrepreneurs identification resulted in eliminating EDP seekers at written test and interview state. Those training institutions which used this method tried to attract maximum number of applicants with a view to have better choice of candidates. Through application blank, *i.e.* first stage of screening, the training organizations sought information about candidates background and ascertained their responses to certain psychological questions. Information provided by the candidates was evaluated as per standardised scoring key. Applicants were then asked to appear in a written behavioural test which usually had tests like 'thematic apperception' test, 'paired comparison' test, test of 'personal efficacy', test of 'locus of control', etc. Based on performance of candidates in written test some candidates got rejected at this stage. Those who performed relatively better qualified for third and final stage of selection, *i.e.* the interview stage. Usually, the interview committee comprised of experts from DICs, state financial corporations, EDPs funding organizations, lead bank in the district, training institutions and small scale industry. The members of the interview committee tried to evaluate each candidate's resources, resourcefulness and aptitude for starting small enterprise. Expert from training institution usually briefed the member of selection committee as to what the interview committee members were required to evaluate at the time of interview. Even though training institutions claimed that they selected persons with entrepreneurial traits and rejected others, but there was no evidence or authentic information so as to agree to this argument. One may have doubts about authenticity/reliability of selection tools and skill of persons who really administered such selection tools for identification of trainees for the EDPs.

There was just one organization which, in addition to interview, gave weightage to project ideas of the applicants. This training organization preferred those candidates for training who had some project ideas of their own.

It is clear from the above discussion that there was no uniformity in entrepreneurs identification process adopted by different training organizations. Also, there were no evidences that institutions which conducted written tests for identification of entrepreneurs achieved better results in comparison to those who did not conduct written tests. Training institutions had apprehension about reliability and authenticity of selection tools and competency of trainers in administering and scoring the selection tests. However, training institutions were unanimous in recommending standardised selection tools which could help in short listing the candidate and identifying entrepreneurial traits among applicants. There is urgent need to train the trainers in making appropriate use of selection tools.

❋❋❋

12

PLANNING FOR FINANCE

Finance is considered as the life-blood of a business as it is the master key which provides access to all sources for being employed in the manufacturing and merchandising activities. The main object of each business is to earn profit for its survival and growth, but in the present-day changing business environment some other objectives like social and national objectives are gaining importance. The proper planning will fulfil these objectives by analysing and forecasting needs, managing working capital, planning capital structure.

Financial Planning. Financial planning is based on the financial appraisal of the projects to be taken up by the management. It is total requirement of long-term and short-term financial requirement of proposed project and then choose the best useful source whose cost is least chosen. Financial planning is useful to an entrepreneur to develop the strategies to set the goals in terms of volumes of profit and sales as well as profit investment: keeping expansion and growth in mind. While deciding the goals, functional ifreas like production, marketing, personnel, inventory management, taxation etc. be given judicious thought.

Steps for Finance Planning

A financial planning should include the following:

1. *Capital Structure.* Determining the capital structure which should he based on a long term planning of the business.

2. *Mode of Financing*. Forecasting the most probable course of events, which may include:

(*a*) Quantum of finance *i.e.,* the amount needed for implementing the business plans;

(*b*) Policies to be pursued for implementing the proposed pattern of financing;

(*c*) Pattern of financing;

(*d*) Time for floating various corporate securities.

The coverage of financial planning: a financial forecast has to be made estimating the under-mentioned elements:

(*a*) Fixed capital requirements.

(*b*) Working capital requirements.

(*c*) Debt-equity ratio.

(*d*) Credit policy to be followed.

(*e*) Other contingencies.

Long-Term and Short-Term Finance Credit Flow

Credit is the prime input for sustained growth of small sector and its availability continues to be a matter of concern. Credit provided for creation of fixed assets like land, building, plant and machinery is called long-term credit. Credit provided for running the industry for its day-to-day requirement for purchasing raw materials and other inputs like electricity and water etc., and for payment of wages and salaries is called short-term credit or working capital. Primary concern of an entrepreneur is to ammge financial resources to take care of all the operational requirements. Such financial resources could be long-term or short-term, which could come from internal or external sources.

The sources of long-term finance include:

(a) Owner's capital *i.e.*, equity.

(b) Term loans from financial institutions.

(c) Deposits or loans given by owners (partners/directors) to the firm.

(d) Hire-purchase or leasing facility from National Small Industries Corporation or other similar organizations.

(e) Machinery purchase under Industrial Development Bank of India's Bill Rediscounting Scheme.

(f) Seed capital, margin money, subsidy, soft loan from Government/Financial Institutions.

The source of short-term finance could be:

(a) Bank borrowing for working capital.

(b) Deposits/borrowing from friends; relatives and others.

(c) Sundry creditors.

(d) Deposits received from customers.

The above are largely external sources for raising finance except owner's capital and loans/deposits from friends and relatives. Funds can be generated internally by the entrepreneur through personal loans on his assets like provident Fund/Life Insurance Corporation/buildings/investments, etc. It could be through personal borrowings from friends and relatives. For a running enterprise, it could be through retention of profits of conversion of assets into foods.

Sound financial management implies that the entrepreneur should plough back a good part of earning into the business enterprise rather than withdrawing the same from the business which will ensure growth and stability. Such a policy will pay rich dividends in future and ensure easy access to bonowing from external sources in times of distress or when the unit is poised for expansion. To ensure sound health, it is essential that short-time funds are utilised by the unit for acquiring current assets like raw materials, stocks in process, finished goods, trade debts, investments, advance to suppliers, etc., *i.e.*, items which are of a current nature and keep changing their shape. They can normally be converted into cash within one year. Higher the current assets, better is the availability of working capital.

On the other hand, long-term finance should be utilised for acquiring fixed assets and partly for financing current assets to meet the margin on working capital.

While arranging funds, the entrepreneur should ensure the cost effectiveness of each source. One must keep in mind the following factors:

(a) Volume of funds required on long-term and short-term basis.

(b) Period for which funds are required.

(c) Time required for obtaining such finance.

(d) Cost of borrowings.

(e) Repayment capacity keeping future profit generation pattern in view.

(f) Conditions stipulated by lenders of money.

The cardinal principle would be to have a mix of funds which works out to be the cheapest, is available most easily and involves minimum outside interference in your day-to-day working. For science and technology entrepreneurs, special loan schemes have been formulated by financial institution and banks including soft loan and equity support. Since these are granted on liberal terms, efforts should be made to use them to the maximum.

Thus, a small-scale enterprise requires two types of finance:

1. *Long-Term Finance.* This is required to buy fixed assets and to maintain minimum working capital. Owners' capital and deposits, term loans from banks and financial institutions, seed capital, margin money and subsidy from Government are the sources of long-term finance.

2. *Short-Term Finance.* Money required to meet day-to-day expenses, to meet seasonal and cyclical variations in the scale of operations, etc. is called short-term finance. Trade creditors, commercial banks, custmner advances, deposits and borrowings from friends and relatives are the main sources.

In order to maintain sound financial health of the enterprise, long term finance should be utilised for acquiring fixed assets and short-term finance should be utilized for acquiring current assets.

Sources of Finance

The various sources of finance may broadly be classified as follows:

Finance

- (A) Internal sources (Ownership capital)
  - *(a)* Equity shares
  - *(b)* Preference shares
  - *(c)* Reinvestment of earnings
  - *(d)* Personal loans
- (B) External sources (Borrowed capital)
  - *(a)* Debentures
  - *(b)* Long-term loans
  - *(c)* Public deposits
  - *(d)* Bank credit

(*e*) Trade credit

(*f*) Hire-purchase and leasing

(*g*) Margin money

(*h*) Seed margin money

Sources of Finance

Internal finance is called ownership capital or equity whereas external finance is known as borrowed capital or debt. In small-scale units owners' equity is generally thin and a major portion of total capital is raised through loans from financial institutions and banks.

Borrowed capital has several advantages. First, the cost of such capital is generally lower than that of equity. Secondly, the owner can retain full control over the enterprise. Thirdly, the money can be repaid as and when not required in business. Lastly, the benefits of trading on equity can be obtained. On the other hand, ownership capital is permanently available. No fixed burden of interest is created and there is no charge on the assets of the enterprise. Generally, fixed capital is financed through equity shares, preference shares, retained earnings, debentures, term loans, leasing and hire purchase.

Characteristics of Small Business Finance

Financing of small business has its unique features; some of these are as:

1. *High Proposition of Working Funds.* Due to labour-intensive technology, a large proportion of total funds is required in the form of liquid assets.

2. *High Gearing.* Generally the ownership funds of the small-scale entrepreneur are limited. He has to depend to a great extent on borrowed funds.

3. *Personal Control.* The entrepreneur wants to retain control of the enterprise. Therefore, he is averse to the sources of funds whereby his control is diluted.

4. *Low Credit Standing.* The creditworthiness of a new small entrepreneur is generally low. He requires credit against the security of his assets.

5. *Poor Documentation.* A small-scale entrepreneur is rarely familiar with legal formalities involved in financing the business. He cannot afford legal experts. Therefore, he prefers few and less time-consuming formalities.

Fixed Capital Management

Each business needs funds for various assets, the need for financial requirement is judged by various assets required by business enterprise. Of course, the structure and quantity of amount will depend upon the nature and size of business unit. An effort should be made to make adequate capital at the time when it is needed.

The capital may be needed:

(a) to pay the purchase consideration;

(b) to support the business operations; and

(c) to meet unexpected/unplanned business expenses.

Estimation. While estimating the capital requirements, the following items should be taken into consideration:

1. *Cost of Promotion.* The expenses incurred on the setting up of the enterprise are called cost of promotion. These include legal and technical fees, cost of survey, expenses of drafting and printing the documents, registration charges, etc.

2. *Cost of Financing.* These consist of printing of application forms and prospectus, advertising expenses for new issue of

shares, underwriting commission, brokerage and other expenses on the marketing of securities.

3. *Cost of Fixed Assets.* Fixed assets are the permanent assets of an enterprise. These include land and buildings, plant and machinery, furniture and fixtures, etc. Capital invested in these assets is known as fixed capital or block capital.

The amount of fixed capital needed for an enterprise depends upon the following factors:

(a) *Nature of Business.* A manufacturing enterprise and a public utility concern require a larger amount of fixed capital as compared to a trading concern.

(b) *Scale of Operations.* A large-scale enterprise generally requires greater fixed capital than a small-scale enterprise. For instance; a large-scale steel enterprise like the Tata Iron and Steel Company requires a huge investment in fixed assets in comparison with a mini-steel plant.

(c) *Type of Manufacturing Process.* Processing (analytical and synthetical) industries generally requite a larger amount of fixed capital than assembly and service industries. Similarly, firms operating in heavy industries like ship-building require more fixed capital than firms operating in light industries, *e.g.*, a sugar plant.

(d) *Mode of Acquiring Fixed Assets.* A firm may buy fixed assets on cash down basis or on hire-purchase and instalment basis. In the latter case the need for fixed capital will be low. Acquiring land and buildings and other fixed assets on lease or hire-purchase basis and sub-contracting production to outside concerns help to reduce the need for fixed capital.

(e) *Technique of Production.* The technique of production also affects the amount of fixed capital. A firm using capital-intensive techniques requires greater fixed capital than another firm of the same size using labour-intensive technology. Shifts in technology lead to changes in the amount of fixed capital.

4. *Cost of Intangible Assets.* Assets like goodwill and patents are called intangible assets. If these are acquired from existing firms, their purchase consideration should be included.

5. *Cost of Developing Business.* The operating losses suffered during the gestation period should be taken into consideration. Contingent expenditure should also be included.

6. *Cost of Current Assets.* Assets like accounts receivable, bills receivable, inventory, cash and bank balances are called current assets. Money invested in thee assets is known as working capital.

Financial Structure or Capital Structure

It is not out of order to suggest an optimum structure of financing, it means the most economical and safe ratio between debt and equity capital. In other words, it is capital mix which is concerned to owner's capital and borrowed funds. A sound financial structure is economical, flexible, simple, safe, balanced and controllable capital mix. The best capital mix is where cost of funds is lowest and the return is comparatively very high. The use of debt capital is not bad but its dangers should not be overlooked.

Determinants of Capital Structure

The following factors should be considered while deciding the debt equity ratio:

1. *Trading on Equity.* It means taking advantage of debt to increase yield on equity. When an enterprise uses borrowed funds along with owned funds, it is said to be trading on

equity. So long as the rate of earnings is greater than the rest of interest payable on debt, there is an advantage in using debt. But the average annual earnings of the enterprise must be sufficient enough to pay interest and repay the debt in time.

2. *Desire to Retain Control.* When the promoters of a company wish to retain control over the company in their own hands, they may raise more funds by issuing preference shares and debentures. The holders of these securities do not enjoy voting rights and, therefore, there is little possibility of loss of control.

3. *Nature of Business.* Companies enjoying regular and liberal earnings *e.g.,* public utilities can afford to have high capital gearing. On the other hand, business firms which are subject to wide fluctuations in demand and earnings may find it safer to depend more on equity capital and preference shares. New and stagnant firms may find it more difficult to issue debentures and preference shares than well-established and growing companies.

4. *Cost of Financing.* In a good financial structure the cost of capital should be reasonably low. Cost of capital depends upon the prevailing rate of interest, return expected by potential investors, issue expenses and administrative expenses. Normally the cost of debt is lower than that of equity. A company should estimate and compare the cost of alternative sources of finance before making a choice among them. High rates of tax make debt financing more attractive.

5. *Need for Flexibility.* Flexibility of financial structure implies the freedom to adapt the capitalization and mix of securities to the changing conditions of business. Equity shares make the capital structure rigid as these cannot generally be paid back before winding up of the company. In order to keep the capital structure elastic a company may issue redeemable preference shares, debentures and public deposits.

These securities are generally not issued in the initial stages of a company as they involve burden of fixed payments and the earnings of a new company.

6. *Period and Purpose of Financing.* For funds required for department investment equity shares are the appropriate choice. Debentures and preference shares are preferable for medium-term finance. Modernization and expansion programmes may better be financed through preference shares and debentures. Finance needed for expansion of capacity may be raised through fixed charge securities as expansion is likely to increase the earning capacity of the company.

7. *Statutory Requirements.* Banking companies are prohibited from issuing any type of security except equity shares. Government of India has laid down norms of debt-equity ratio and ceiling on public deposits. Thus, state regulations regarding the issue of securities have a bearing on capital structure.

8. *Capital Market Conditions.* The state of capital market influences the choice of securities to be issued. During boom investors are willing to take risk and invest in equity shares. But in a bearish market, of down swing investors prefer safe investment. Therefore, preference shares and debentures carrying a fixed rate of return are likely to be more marketable in a depression.

9. *Need of Investors.* Investors' attitudes and requirements regarding income and risk is an important consideration in designing capital structure. A company may issue securities of different kinds and varying denominations to meet the likings of potential investors. Enterprising investors who prefer capital gains and a say in the management of the company can be lured by issuing equity shares. Debentures and preference shares are issued to attract investors who desire a regular return and safety of investment.

Estimation (Assessment) of Working Capital

The working capital is needed for the following:

(a) Purchase of raw materials and consumable stores needed by the enterprise.

(b) Work-in-progress (some manufactured goods).

(c) Finished goods.

(d) Trade debtors (bills receivables).

(e) Expenses.

The elements of current assets are as:

Management of Working Capital. Working capital management is a significant facet of financial management. It is important that the investment in current assets and the level of current liabilities will have to be geared quickly to changes in sales. It is also important that a portion of the working capital requirement is brought from long-term sources such as equity capital or long-term loans.

Part of the total capital employed in a business has to be deployed in financing current assets. Ignoring cash, the main current assets are: stock-in-trade and trade debtors. On the other hand, the current liabilities of the business reduce the amount of the capital which the business has to provide to finance its operations. The main current liabilities are trade creditors and bank overdraft. Excess of current assets over current liabilities is working capital.

(1) *Raw Materials and Consumables.* Funds requirements for holding raw materials depends on:

(a) Average consumption of raw material,

(b) Fluctuations in the raw material consumption (depends on whether the items ate regularly consumed or bulk quantities are required at a time).

(*c*) Fluctuations in the raw material availability,

(*d*) Minimum quantities supplied by the market,

(*e*) Storage facility available,

(*f*) Criticality of an item (*i.e.* how important an item is in order to maintain production).

This raw material requirements is generally expressed as 'so many months requirement'. To illustrate, if the raw material consumption in a year is Rs. 1,20,000 and depending on the various considerations listed above, if it is considered that 2 months raw materials will have to be kept for Rs. 10,000 as given below:

(Rs. 1,20,000 ÷ 12 months) × 2 months = Rs. 20,000

(2) *Work-in-Process.* The funds blocked up in work-in-process depend on the following factors:

(*a*) Time required for conversion of raw materials.

(*b*) Average quantities of each product processed at each time (batch quantity).

(*c*) Number of products handled at a time in the process.

(*d*) The process, *i.e.*, the manner in which raw materials are added in the process.

To illustrate, the major raw materials in the case of a grey iron foundry are added in the initial stages while in an assembly unit, as in TV industry, the major raw materials and components are added at the last stage of the process.

Hence funds requirement for work-in-process depends upon

– Value of raw materials in semi-finished components products.

– Value added at each stage.

In case, where a number of components are involved, the general practice of valuation of working process is given by raw materials + ½ (value added) *i.e.*, it is assumed that the materials have undergone half the processing where value added = selling price – profit – material cost.

(3) *Finished Goods.* Goods may be manufactured against firm orders or against anticipated orders. In the former case the quantum of finished goods held depends on:

(a) Delay due to inspection of the finished goods especially where an external agency is involved.

(b) Delay in preparation of dispatch documents.

(c) Delays due to non-availability of wagons.

(d) Delays in shipment.

(e) Minimum quantity that can be dispatched (*e.g.*, full truck load).

In the case of goods manufactured to stock against anticipated orders, the quantity of finished goods held depends on:

(a) Average dispatch quantity of finished goods.

(b) Minimum quantities that can be dispatched.

(c) Variation due to sudden requirement or slump in the market.

(d) Delays due to non-availability of transport vehicles, trucks, wagons, etc.

The requirement of working funds against blocked up finished goods is expressed as 'so many days production'. The valuation of finished goods is at the full cost of production of the product.

(4) *Trade Debtors (Accounts Receivable).* If all sales were made for cash there would be no need to employ part of the

capital of the business in financing debtors. Debtors arise as the result of sales made on credit. The amount of capital employed in financing debtors depends on the period for which credit is given and on the efficiency of the collection process at the end of this period. The main points to consider are:

(a) That appropriate terms are agreed in advance with customers and then enforced;

(b) That the necessary invoices, statements, reminders, etc. are prepared and dispatched promptly;

(c) That the following alternative possibilities of providing finance have been considered:

— offering discounts for prompt payment;

— using factoring services;

— using credit collection agencies.

Discounts, factoring services and credit collection agencies are, however, expensive. Except in a tight liquidity situation the costs may outweigh the benefits.

It is, however, in the case of credit sales that working funds are required to meet delays in sales realization. The quantum of working funds required depends on the period of credit given. The computation of the value of the working funds is based on the cost of production.

(5) *Expenses.* It is generally expected that about one month's requirement of cash expenses is required to be kept in the form of cash for meeting out contingencies like fluctuations in material prices, delays in sales realization, etc. The quantum of such cash retention fur meeting working capital requirements depends upon the process time. For activities having long processing time like ship-building, higher quantum of such cash balance has to be retained.

The format for consumption of working capital requirements and bank finance is shown later.

Sources of Working Capital Requirements

Working capital needs of a unit are financed from various sources as follows:

(1) *Own Funds.* Regulations for financing of working capital needs by financial institutions stipulate a certain stake of the borrower to ensure proper management of funds. This stake of the owner, otherwise termed, 'Margin Money', is what comes out of the equity or own funds of the borrower. Thus, the owner's funds go partly to meet the expenses towards acquisition of assets like land, building, etc., and partly as 'margin' towards working capital needs.

(2) *Other Short-Term Finance.* Industries in general also get credit for some of the expenses on a continuous basis. About 45 days credit is available on power bills, about 15 days in the case of wages paid monthly, etc. In addition, units also get advance for supplies.

(3) *Sundry Creditors.* Creditors available against purchase of materials go to meet the working capital needs. To cite an illustration, a small scale unit is engaged in cloth printing on a job work basis where the customer himself gives the cloth to be printed. The unit gets about one month credit on purchase of dyes and chemicals for printing while many a time printing is completed in a week's time and the printing charges collected within 15 days.

Thus, the unit is able to effectively finance the entire working capital needs from sundry creditors.

(4) *Bank Borrowings.* By and large a major portion of the working funds is financed by the banker because of the following reasons:

(*a*) Within a prescribed limit, working capital funds can be availed of as per requirements.

(*b*) The limit itself can be altered depending on the activity level.

(*c*) The rate of interest is reasonable compared to other borrowings.

(5) *Short-Term Borrowings.* Working capital requirements fluctuate on a day-to-day basis depending on exigencies. Therefore, occasions do arise when the unit has to resort to short term borrowing from friends, or other market sources. This happens because the various other sources are not adequate enough to meet the requirements.

(6) *Management of Cash.* A reference of the working cycle shows that the surplus generated in each cycle is not withdrawn from the cycle. This surplus shows itself over a number of cycles as cash. The cash position of the unit, however, does not truly reflect the surplus position. Sometimes it shows itself as surplus whereas it is really meant for payment during subsequent months. This situation arises in cases where expenses are incurred on a specified data, *e.g.*, sales tax, bonus, income tax, etc. Hence, it is necessary to clearly identify the quantum of real surplus and those that are required to meet future expenditure. Diversion of short-term funds for long purposes due to shortsightedness of the management has been noticed in a number of units. Tins results in insufficient availability of working funds thereby crippling the activities. It is not hard to visualise a situation where for want of sufficient working funds, a unit slowly grinds to a halt.

A judicious combination of the different sources of funds should be employed so that sufficient funds are raised at the cheapest cost.

❋❋❋

INDEX

F

G

H